MY *Intuition*
MADE ME DO IT

A. K. BIRD

My Intuition Made Me Do It

Copyright © 2024 by A. K. Bird

All rights reserved. No part of this book may be reproduced, distributed, or transmitted in any form or by any means, including photocopying, recording, or other electronic or mechanical methods, without the prior written permission of the author except in the case of uses permitted by copyright law. For permission requests, write to the author at the webpage below.

www.authorakbird.com/pages/contact

Library and Archives Canada Cataloguing in Publication:
[ISBN: 978-1-0689965-0-4]

Publisher: A. K. Bird

Cover design by: David Gardias, Best Selling Covers

Contents

	The Journey	3
1.	Love at Steak	21
2.	Intro to Tarot	35
3.	Two Little Things	45
4.	Three Little Things	59
5.	Audacious Dawn	73
6.	Breakup Words	87
7.	Blocking of One's Path	109
8.	A Cosmic Ultimatum	121
9.	Pratibha's Path	125
10.	The Good Birthday	137
11.	Eight of Swords	153
12.	Ribs vs. Ribcages	167
13.	Summer Solstice	171
14.	I Am a Leader	193

This story is written in a style called *roman á clef*. It's a french term meaning 'novel with a key'.

The key being: you would have needed to be there to know.

The events and interactions which follow are based in truth and lived experience. Certain character arcs, timelines, and other elements have been fictionalized to maintain story flow and consistency.

Rustles & Comfort

Reflected Heat

Sweeping Entrance

Swiftly The Jet

I Wait for the Drum

The Voice & The Drum

Lull Me in Waking Sleep

The Journey

The familiar outline of the sidewalk was barely visible. Rain laced with fragments of ice poured from the sky and my glasses were streaked with water. The hazy glare of streetlights reflected on the pavement in rippling shadows. Black and burnt orange painted the night in a heavy glow.

I had made the walk from my car, parked up a hill two blocks away to the yoga studio, many times in the last few months. Tonight, I ran.

My pace this evening held a sense of urgency not caused by the frigid downpour. I knew there was going to be a shift tonight. There had to be.

I had been asking, pleading, praying for change.

My hand grasped the door to the yoga studio and pulled it open. A rush of warm air greeted me and filled my senses with the smell of smoke and lemongrass. My glasses instantly fogged, and all I could see were bright and neutral tones.

The contrast to outside was startling.

The intense spattering of raindrops hitting concrete quieted to a muffled patter as the door shut behind me.

Unzipping my jacket, I took my glasses off to wipe them on the soft shirt beneath my sweater.

As I rubbed the lenses, my eyes settled on the blurry shapes of the altar that greeted every patron of the studio. A hollow blue triangle with a brown line in its centre ended in a dot of bright red. Flickering yellow orbs flared against a backdrop of indistinct white and purple shapes.

When the water drops had absorbed and streaks had been minimized, I returned my glasses to my face. I could see a curl of grey rising from the tip of the incense in the blue temple. The candles had flames now, and quartz and amethyst crystals appeared carefully placed within and around the temple, honouring all who would practice.

Pleased I could see again, I second-guessed my choice to leave my contacts at home. If the effort I put into my appearance before leaving the house was any indication of my state of well-being, 'well' would be a stretch.

My blonde hair had air-dried into its natural unkempt waves, I wore leggings I picked up off the floor of the bedroom, and I could give myself credit for swiping mascara onto my lashes before I left the house. Another mistake for tonight, I was sure.

I pulled my phone out of my pocket to check the time, silently hoping a text would appear on my screen as my thumb tapped it awake.

Nothing.

The silent treatment continued.

After removing my soaked footwear, I approached the desk to sign in.

A slight girl with large hoop earrings and an asymmetrical pixie cut welcomed me. "Hey there! Are you here for the Shamanic Journey?"

The girl had been at the front desk for a few of my previous classes and always had a kind, approachable vibe. I had yet to ask her name.

"Hello!" I returned her greeting. Reaching for the tablet that I usually used to sign in, I asked, "Is this the first time it's been offered?"

"It is! Have you already registered for the class?"

I scrolled down the list until I found my name.

"Yes, I registered as soon as I saw it." The comment gave away my excitement, which I attempted to stifle as I multitasked politely and made the selections to sign in for class.

The girl looked down at her own tablet as I completed the sign-in.

"You're in for such an experience. This is the first time Leila has offered it to us, but I've heard it's been transformational at other events." She pointed down the hallway behind her. "Well, Hallie, I hope you enjoy. You'll be in the Ishvara Shala tonight. It's the small one to your left."

I smiled as I moved toward the hall. "Thank you!"

The room that had 'Ishvara'— a Sanskrit word meaning 'higher consciousness'—written on its door was around the first corner on my way to the ladies' change rooms. I could already picture the 'Shala'—a

Sanskrit word meaning 'home'—from my previous classes at the studio. It was small and square, with miniature windows just below the ceiling to let in light from the lobby. The lights were never turned on, giving this room a gentle ambiance and a relaxing atmosphere.

I continued walking until I reached the change room, making my way to a corner of the hooks and benches lining the space. After depositing my backpack on the bench I hung my jacket, happy to be free of the stuffy and damp encasing.

From my backpack, I took out my rolled yoga mat. It was glistening from exposure to the rain. I wiped the sleeve of my sweater on the outside of the mat but determined it a useless attempt.

I also retrieved my journal, a pen, and my favourite quartz crystal. I grasped my crystal tightly. It had joined me throughout my sessions at this studio and felt like a dear friend I could confess all my fears and dreams to. The crystal was clear and smooth and fit perfectly in the palm of my hand. It was shaped like the grip of a dagger, only missing its blade.

My emotional state was as numb as my toes. Fortunately, both felt more sensation now that my environment had shifted and warmed.

As I entered the shala, a ring of a dozen bolsters and blankets had already been set up. Candles were lit at the edges of the room and in a cluster in the centre. Their flickering danced on the walls as I danced around the circle of mats to arrive at my desired spot. Sidestepping the other attendees, I found myself in the far corner of the room.

I unrolled my mat.

A few raindrops still spattered and speckled the upper surface of it. Instead of wiping them away, I embraced the fact that the thin layer of water would dry in the warmth of the room.

I prepared my blocks and set the bolster on top of them in such a way that the long cushion was propped into an incline. I then turned to my journal and pen which had been deposited beside the blanket.

Shifting my attention to the room, I observed the others who walked in and began to set up for their meditation as well. A man with curly hair wove through the mats, nearly tripping over a girl my age who sat directly across from me. Eventually, he found a space he liked and sat a few mats to my left. My eyes pinched in amusement as I witnessed the scene.

Everyone attending the class was settling in.

I wrote a few words which came to my mind in my journal. The pages prior to the one where the tip of my pen currently formed a creative, slanting script were filled with gratitude and grievances of the last several months. Most of it was an elegant, loopy scribble.

Poetry was always cursive.

The glimmer of dark hair caught my eye. Leila entered the room and sat at the first space in the circle; a spot reserved by a sheepskin rug. She was tall and dark, with silky black hair reaching her waist. The shadows of the candlelight dimly reflected strong features as she shifted, her beaded necklace swinging while she moved into a cross-legged seat. From her bag, she pulled a hand-bound drum and mallet which she placed at her side.

I put my pen and journal down, settling into a matching posture just in front of the incline I created. The atmosphere of the room held a respectful silence until the woman spoke.

"As we sit, with our spines connecting us to the earth below, we recognize the nations who took care of this land before our yoga studio came to reside upon it. May we honour them."

I extended wordless appreciation and felt a deep sense of calm. Calling to mind the land's original keepers felt like a necessary practice. Our facilitator's offering was rooted in shamanic practices, and tonight I was being gifted an opportunity to experience it.

She held a pause before formally addressing the class.

"Welcome. Tonight is going to be a Journey into a new chapter for each of you. I often allow you to set your own intentions, but tonight I am going to set one for you. For anyone who has come to my Nidra class but who has not yet come to the Shamanic Journey, this is going to be a little different. This, is sacred."

Her tone held a comforting cadence. She was soft spoken yet commanding with her words. My heart felt heavy in my chest, though I could not pinpoint its cause other than a growing anticipation of what was to come.

I am Love.

The Yoga Nidra class Leila had offered since the fall had become my refuge. In Nidra, it is often instructed to create a Sankalpa. This is a short, concise, 'I Am' statement which is said to have the ability to settle into our subconscious and make lasting change in our lives.

At the first Nidra class I attended, I cried as I formed my Sankalpa: 'I am Love'. It was an effort to cultivate more of the affection and patience my boyfriend was so desperately asking me for.

At the beginning of each Nidra class, Leila introduced the theory of the practice. Nidra means 'yogic sleep' and the depth of this style of meditation allows our brain states to shift from beta waves, which is our normal conscious thinking state, into the alpha and sometimes even theta wave states associated with dreamlike visions. Leila specialized in accessing these subconscious states.

In my first class, we were told the intentions we set would present us with a major shift near the end of February. It's the beginning of March now. I was certain tonight would be the catalyst for the shift my soul needed.

I wanted to be a good partner. I wanted my boyfriend to feel loved. I didn't know what I was doing wrong...

What began as minor misunderstandings between us where I calmly attempted to articulate my feelings and thoughts with care and maturity escalated to unhinged screams escaping my vocal cords last night.

I was trying, and trying, and trying to shift what we had into something healthier, but a threshold had been breached and a soul I no longer recognized had surfaced.

"Ritual is an important practice as it symbolically lets the subconscious know that we are coming into ceremony. I have sage for cleansing ourselves of anything attached to us which is not ours. This practice tonight is all about you."

A flash of opalescence caught my attention. Leila lifted an abalone shell from her sheepskin rug. A small bundle of sage was held in the hollow curve of the shell's spiraled centre. She lit the herb with a lighter and passed the abalone shell to a young man sitting to her left.

"You may pull the smoke toward you, almost as though you are washing yourself with it. Perhaps you will scoop it over your head or bring it into your heart. There is every right way to smudge and no way to make an error. As long as you embrace the knowledge that you are clearing your spirit, your spirit will be cleared."

The girl sitting across from me accepted the shell. Soft, twirling smoke rose from the dish and caressed her face. Gently cradling the shell with one hand, her other hand scooped the smoke in rhythmic motions toward her pelvis, navel, heart, throat, brow, and finally over her head. She was clearing her chakra centres, the clusters of spiritual energy in our bodies.

An earthly scent drifted between us. It was smoky, more pleasant than a cigarette and sweeter than a campfire. I was calmed by the fragrance and the tension held in my shoulders softened.

"I'd like to ask who here is connected to their guides?"

To my surprise, half the students raised their hands.

Guides? I had been going to Nidra for four months and I had never felt led by anything or anyone. Was I missing something? I had not heard of guides and had not experienced their presence before.

"Before we settle down for the Journey, we're going to ask our guides for protection. It will not matter if you are not connected to them or are not aware of them. Everyone has guides with them, always. As you begin to settle into a comfortable position, I would ask you to invoke the feeling of gratitude. Be grateful to your Self for coming tonight, and for the care you will receive by allowing your spirit to practice. Call in gratitude for everything which may have led you here to this moment."

I was open to these 'guides' and believed that any benevolent spirits accompanying me were welcome.

I was next in the circle to smudge. Accepting the sage my neighbour offered me, I smiled at her as I took the abalone shell into my hands. Smoke rose from the smouldering embers, curling gently over the sides of the dish.

The sharp edges of the shell chafed on my dry palms. Enamoured by the multicoloured shimmer which coated the inner ridges, I watched as streams of smoke folded over each other in such a way that they looked like lovers quarrelling.

I would know. I was one such lover.

Cupping my hands, I let the smoke pool into my palms. The smoke barely caused sensation against my skin as I lifted it over my shoulders. The weighted air washed away a staleness I was only aware of now my attention focused on clearing it away. I pulled the tendrils over my arms and legs then, mimicking the girl across from me, pulled the smoke toward each of my chakras. I let the smoke linger at my third eye, breathing in deeply and praying for clarity.

I didn't have to evoke a feeling of gratitude as I cleansed myself with the smoke. It was already there. My soul knew I was exactly where I needed to be: here at the studio. Before leaving the house, I had hesitated on the doorstep, not wanting to brave the rain and the cold but knowing this may be my last chance to resolve the turmoil within me.

"Call upon your guides and ask them to release and protect you from anything which does not serve you or help you grow. Ask to be guided by Spirit tonight, for she has important insight to bring you."

May I be protected as I Journey and released from anything which does not serve me. May I be guided by spirit to bring me to the answers I most need to hear.

I set the intention into my subconscious and passed the abalone shell to my left.

"When we string our drums, we infuse them with intention. This drum has a masculine energy, it is here to 'Untangle Knots'. The intention I will set for us all tonight is: 'Reveal to me the truth I need to hear'"

The bowl of sage passed through each person, returning to Leila.

"Lay back now and find comfort. We will begin in a moment."

At her cue, everyone began to settle back and lay down. I had learned comfort was infinitely important in the Nidra classes, as laying so still for the hour caused odd and small places on the body to experience big and distracting sensations. Therefore, I took extra care in lining up my bolster before laying back.

I placed my glasses near the top edge of my mat, deeming it to be the safest place. Closing my eyes, I balanced the quartz in the curve of my sternum, nestling it into the soft bulk of my sweater. I lifted the blanket over myself before shuffling and shifting until I was in the most comfortable position I could achieve.

Reveal to me the truth I need to hear.

As I repeated the collective intention, Leila began to drum.

The drum was loud and vibrated through the entirety of my body, becoming especially resonant in the centre of my chest. My eyes became heavier as I lost myself in the sound. I focused my attention into the darkness between my eyes and waited.

"If you can't accept the love I'm offering, I don't know what more I can do!"

The words had escaped in a desperate cry as I walked out of the bedroom at 1:30 in the morning last night, slamming the door behind me. I don't think I had ever slammed a door before, and walking out to the living space alone with my partner reeling from my words in the bedroom we shared felt like I had betrayed a core element of my Self.

Convinced my outburst had left a deep wound, I felt a knot of guilt tighten in my stomach. How had I allowed this discord to grow into such a rage?

I wanted to be peaceful. To be patient. To demonstrate my best attempt at emotional maturity...

Anger had lodged itself between us, and I didn't know how to get around the obstacle it had formed.

It had been building inside me for weeks, these past twenty-four hours being especially treacherous

> I'm sorry for not having better communication skills to mend the bridge like I hoped. I'm sorry for slamming the door on you.

The texted apology I sent earlier that afternoon had gone unanswered.

What was I doing wrong?

As I lay in the dimly lit room, I couldn't shake the nagging fear that my actions had driven a permanent wedge between us. Could our relationship survive this fracture, or had my outburst shattered something too precious to repair?

Shaking the focus from my fears, I returned it to centre. I wasn't here to Journey to keep ruminating over my circumstances. I had done enough of that already.

Leila had started the drums with a slow rhythm, with alternating tones and depths of vibration which had begun building at a steady pace. The moderate tempo settled in my ribcage.

My breathing slowed into a relaxed cadence as I recalled the night's intention.

Behind my eyes, the colour red bloomed from the darkness.

At first it started as a smoky haze, but soon my surroundings formed.

In this room—the Ishvara Shala—decorated with the same mats all in a circle, I sat at the top of my mat. The men who had filtered into the room at the beginning of class no longer sat in the spaces they had occupied. Elder and youthful faces graced this new circle of women.

The dimly lit space, now cast in a red light, reminded me of a dark room where photographs were developed. The ambiance heightened my anxiety, but I remained willing to embrace the unfolding of my vision.

I looked at the women in the circle. They were talking joyously to each other, passing around fabrics and trinkets to show. None of them seemed to be aware of my presence.

Why was I unseen?

Suddenly, my vision shifted.

In front of me, cast in the same red ambiance, sat a young girl. Her hair looked black in contrast to the red light and her head tilted down in such a way that I could not see her features.

As I looked at the young girl, a strange yet undeniable connection to her settled in my chest. I *knew* her. She was familiar, but not in a manner I could pinpoint. Her posture timid, yet there was a quiet strength emanating from her, and I couldn't help but be drawn to her presence.

Something like a gravitational pull at my growing interest prompted me to reach out an unsteady hand.

Inspired by Leila's words at the start of class, within the vision I asked the girl, "are you my guide?"

The moment I asked the question and before my fingers brushed the girl's shoulder, a blackened abyss overwhelmed me.

No more vision.

No more light.

Only a vast expanse of nothingness presented behind the lids of my eyes.

Startled and confused, I took that as a harsh 'no', and a redirection.

Okay, I thought. *Relax and accept the messages as they come.*

I softened the tension of my thoughts and once again attempted to relax into the centre of my mind. I spent a couple moments in the darkness before noticing I was exceptionally still, finally. Reminding myself of my intention, I began to focus on why I was there to Journey.

The bright green eyes of my partner came to mind.

The moment his firm brow and kind face appeared in my vision, an abrupt rushing sensation slammed a barrier down behind my eyes.

Anxiously, I reached out to feel the invisible force with my mind's eye. My envisioned hands extended slowly, feeling nothing until unexpectedly a frigid sensation akin to touching a frosted windowpane connected with my fingertips. I could feel an unmoving wall before me, sending shivers up my arms.

The wall seemed to hum with a low, haunting vibration like there was an energy behind it. Something great, something vibrant was behind this barrier but I could not claim to know what it was.

As my surroundings shifted, I found myself standing in a deep blue, darkened cave. The cool dampness of the air wrapped around me like a heavy cloak. The barrier before me now appeared like a thick, frosted, icy window, casting distorted shadows that danced across the uneven walls. It was the only source of light, reflecting off edges and curves in the walls around me. The colours and shapes behind the barrier morphed and shifted. It was a mesmerizing play of light. I could sense a powerful presence beyond the icy veil, radiating an energy that was both magnetic and unnerving.

I reached out to touch the barrier once more, feeling the cold, crystalline surface against my fingertips, the sensation chilling me. The humming kept tempo with the drumming oscillating in my ears. The icy window seemed to throb with each drumbeat, holding an anticipation as if it was guarding a secret, waiting for the moment when the veil would be lifted.

I attempted to envision this mysterious, invisible wall dissipating, hoping to see what lie in the lively other side. I prayed for a solution to the strife with my partner.

Blackness.

All the light of my visionary environment disappeared.

I tried again to envision my partner's image. The sturdy features that attracted me to him. The broad shoulders that held me tightly over the past three years.

This time, it was as though he was blinding galaxies and starscapes away from me, the distance between us echoing with the emptiness of space. He was on the other side of my mental universe, an infinitesimal figure in the long, black tunnel of my consciousness.

I tried to call him in closer, but his image wouldn't come any nearer. I could not hold him in my space.

You, alone.

The message rose from deep within.

You, alone.

A tightness pierced my chest, and my next breath caught in a hitch. My rising anxiety nearly prevented my next inhale.

I believed if I could be better, more understanding, more patient, then I could salvage the love we once shared. Every time we argued, every time I felt the distance between us grow, I turned inward.

I didn't *want* to be alone.

A deep, shaky breath escaped my lips.

I needed something to ground into.

Focusing on the space between my brows, I let my mind relax again. I fell into a state of trust in my path and allowed myself to be guided.

There had to be a reason why Spirit was calling me to do this.

What plan do you have for me to make this worth it?

I took three deep breaths as I asked the question and chose to lose myself in the reverberations I felt in my chest. I surrendered to the drum. The deep, rhythmic sound was oscillating through my soul. Every pound on the drum was a beat struck through my heart. In the undertone of the deepest notes I could hear wind dancing and swirling through trees.

Lush, green mountains surrounded me. Peaks shrouded in mist created an ethereal atmosphere. They blocked my view of the sky, standing sturdy with their coats of conifers. Each tree stood like a sentinel, protecting the secrets of the mountains they called home.

Banff.

I had plans to go there already.

Tickets had been purchased for the Pratibha Yoga Festival in May. I had bought a pair of them so that I could attend with my best friend.

The scene shifted and a flash of images started to flicker through my mind.

A yellow bike on a beach with palm trees. A steaming mug of chai in a trendy cafe. The floating whispers of feathers in the wind. The flashing lights of a festival's stage. Two glasses of wine clinking in a vineyard. Myself, sitting at the edge of a stream with a set of singing bowls, playing sweet songs for the water.

The visions ceased as the last beat fell on the drum.

Tears were already falling down my cheeks as I lay unmoving in the break of silence which followed. I could feel them running down my temples and into my hair.

Leila closed the class.

I could hardly concentrate on the words she was saying. She usually closed our Nidra class by asking us to take some time before driving and drinking water when we got home. Tonight I could not hear her words and instead focused on my breath.

Movement stirred.

The class began to collect their belongings and leave. I remained still and listened for the moment the last person left the room.

The shala was quiet. The candles, still flickering, were the only company of my internal panic. The moment my mind wandered, the absolute turmoil of last night caught up to me.

I just cried.

Raw emotion flowed from my eyes and rapidly followed the curve of my temple into my hairline. I didn't even move to break the tributary of my tears. I let it dampen my face, wet my hair, and collect in the cartilage of my ears.

A knock on the door broke me of my distress.

The girl at reception was at the door of the shala.

"Hi there, we just need to start cleaning the studio. No need to rush out, but our karma cleaners have to reset the room," She said gently.

I blinked my eyes awake through dense, wet lashes and rolled off the bolster onto my side.

Big sigh.

After a moment I unhurriedly folded my blanket, went through the motions of gathering my belongings, and began to roll up my mat. Putting my blocks and bolsters away, I assembled my things and left the shala.

The studio's volunteers were wiping mats as I headed to the change rooms. One of them gave me an empathetic smile. I did my best attempt to return the expression, but it wasn't a genuine gesture.

I collected my backpack and jacket but was no longer present. Caught in a dazed trance, I numbed my emotional reaction to the night's experience.

"Take care tonight, it's icy!" The girl at reception called as I put on my shoes.

Nodding, my hand waved on autopilot toward the front desk. I opened the door to the studio and walked out into the cold and dark night.

The rain, now misting lightly, coated my face in a damp moisture as I left the studio. I walked slowly to my car, knowing that every step I took was a step closer to needing to face my partner who waited at home.

When I reached my vehicle I sat for a moment, allowing it to idle and warm. Turning my music to a gentle playlist, I checked my reflection in the rearview mirror.

My mascara had settled on my lower lash line in a blackened motif. Salt stained my cheeks, leaving a trail of rough crystals extending from the corners of my eyes.

I licked my thumb and attempted to wipe away the evidence of my distress. With some effort, I was able to fix the mascara, but there was no hope for the puffy redness that gave me away.

Shaking my head, I pulled away from my parking spot.

The drive home seemed to take hours rather than the few short minutes spent in light traffic. Remaining focused on the road considering that it was slick with ice, I allowed my playlist to calm me. Grateful for each stoplight, the red glow served to prolong my drive home and allow me to remain in this state of unfeeling. Eventually, I navigated into the back driveway, parked, and stared at the house.

I unlocked my phone with my thumbprint, heading straight for the album of photos I kept of my relationship.

The first, the night we met. At a music event on Valentine's Day, his friends had abandoned him and I drove him home. In the photo I'm already wearing his flannel tied around my waist, obscuring a fishnet and booty short ensemble. He has a hat I picked up off the floor because I liked the sunflowers on the brim of it held in his hand.

Another, at a festival in B.C, against a chain-link fence where my hair is in its natural waves. I'm wearing a bucket hat and he's wearing a hydration pack with the bite valve hanging against his chest. We look happy.

A screenshot from the same festival, where we had separated to see different artists and the crowds were obnoxiously dense:

He had gifted us that trip to B.C. because he knew my favourite artist would be there. His attentiveness to my desires was always one of the things that drew me to him. I hadn't even expressed interest in the festival; somehow he just knew. Perhaps from spending time with my playlist, perhaps because this was the first time they were anywhere nearby for as long as I had listened to their work. Regardless, it was one of his gifts that enamoured me dearly.

After several minutes, I wiped my eyes one last time. I couldn't stay out all night, as much as I was inclined to do so.

I opened the gate to the backyard and slowly followed the pavers along the fence to the door.

There was no entering silently.

The welcoming howl of our pup greeted me as I unlocked and opened the door.

The entire lower half of his black, streamlined body rippled like a lever, rapidly twisting from side to side.

"Hi Rigs," I whispered as I crept inside and quietly took off my shoes. Riggley waited for me to descend the stairs of our basement suite, anxiously wiggling at the bottom step.

Proud of him for waiting, my hand met his soft head for a few strokes before taking a sharp right and opening the door to our bedroom. I had been working on his front door behaviour for several weeks and we were showing consistent improvement over the last few days. The goal was to have him sit until I made it to the bottom, but I was happy enough with him not charging up to greet me.

Riggley followed me as I tucked my journal away in the drawer of my night table silently. As I closed the drawer and straightened, a voice in the doorway jarred my senses.

"How was class?" He had heard me come in. After our icy interactions, I was surprised at the bid on connection.

My eyes lifted to greet him and it only took a glance at my face for him to know something was wrong.

"Hey, what's the matter? It's okay." His dark brows creased and his full lips tensed. I could hear the concern in his voice.

I could already feel the tears returning to my eyes and a constriction starting in my throat. All I could do was walk past our pup and forward into him, nestling myself into his strong arms. He put his hand on the back of my head and waited for a response.

"Tonight was hard. I went to a class, and it brought up something I'm just not sure how to handle yet," I mumbled into his shoulder once I had a moment to find my voice.

"Okay, it's alright. Can I do anything to help?"

"Just be patient with me please, that's all."

"Okay, I can do that. Always." He pulled me an arm's length away from him to look me in the eye. "It's going to be okay."

"Thank you, Jordan."

Love at Steak

A KISS ON THE forehead and a cup of tea placed on the corner of my night table stirred me from my morning sleep.

"Have a great day, Sweetheart," Jordan whispered.

"Love you," I mumbled sleepily.

"You too," he said as he left for work.

I stayed curled in bed until my tea had gone cold and the sun had passed the brightest point in the room. Eventually, though, it was time to get up.

Jordan worked out of town for a few days at a time, this time for a two-day shift. I didn't mind that he worked away from home. I felt like it gave me time to be independent, but I also was struggling somewhat with my own daily cycles.

My typical routine was to watch movies, take Riggley to the park, and sporadically nap throughout the day when I didn't have an active job to do. I wasn't proud of it, but an internal war against a constant state of exhaustion and my lacking sense of purpose had been raging since the new year.

I worked as a freelance videographer, video editor, and graphic designer. This paid the bills and then some with most of my clients being local businesses in need of marketing. I had done a big job over the holidays which I could comfortably float off of for the next few months and wasn't feeling like spending my time on marketing my services to secure the next client.

I rose from the bed as Rigs raised his head from his spot at my feet.

"Time to get up, Sir," I told him. He did no such thing, just wagged his tail with muffled thuds patting the bed.

I leaned over, giving him a kiss on the top of his head. His sweet black Aussie-Lab face grinned back at me, reminding me of the bottom tooth we lost last week playing ball at the park.

Glancing at the tea, I regretted letting it go cold.

I walked over to the long, half-height wardrobe at the foot of our bed and began to get dressed. My mood seemed improved from last night and this was reflected in my choice of outfit. I selected a pair of jeans and one of my nicer shirt and cardigan sets. Once dressed, I gathered my journal, a blanket, and some incense into my designated "adventure pack".

My pen slipped out of my hand as my fingers made contact with it and fell onto the dark grey carpet. It somehow bounced under the side of the bed. As I got down on my hands and knees to find it, my face was assaulted by Riggleys tongue. Laughing at his opportunism, I found my pen, one of Rigs' rubber balls, and a few dust bunnies.

I handed the ball to Riggley who promptly left the room with it between his teeth. Collecting the pen, I followed him into our living area.

My feet padded on cold grey tile as I made my way from the primary bedroom at the back of our basement suite to the kitchen at the front.

I turned on a switch in the hallway and the pot lights illuminating the light grey walls of my hallway made my eyes blink twice at the brightness.

Passing the hall closet, the bathroom, and spare room I headed for the fridge, the first appliance to demarcate the kitchen from the hallway. I opened the white door which coloured at the bottom with the stain of spray-paint coated rust and took assessment of my options.

Yogurt. A few cups of yogurt, a half-carton of grape tomatoes, and a sprig of parsley. We needed groceries.

I closed the fridge, returning down the hall to the closet. I tucked my favourite quartz crystal and my cell phone into the outer pocket of my heaviest coat, lifting my adventure pack over my shoulder.

The moment he heard the jingle of keys, Riggley was at my side from where I could only assume was his crate.

"Time for a walk?" I asked, gathering his retractable leash, coat, and bags. Excited yelps came from behind the closet door.

Once I had collected everything, I closed the door. Riggley settled for me to put his red buffalo plaid raincoat on, excited whimpers coming in high-pitched tones.

Once the coat was secured, I stood and found stillness at the bottom of the stairs.

I waited.

The shadow circling my legs was a chaotic, squirming, softly yelping and whining pup. He knew the routine, and his hind almost grazed the tile a few times over the course of a minute.

I waited.

No command, no hand signal, just silence and patience.

After a few moments of my calm, inactive behaviour, Riggley began to calm, too.

A sit.

I took a breath before taking a step forward... Then promptly returned my foot back to where it was.

Rigs' lifted figure returned to a sit. I stepped forward again.

This was our game. He had to be sitting as I walked up the stairs, put my shoes on, and opened the door or else I would return to the bottom landing and we would try again.

He stared at me eagerly as I ascended the stairs and slipped on a pair of runners. He leaned forward as I opened the door. I stepped out of the doorway which was normally where he lost it. Today, though, he remained sitting at the base of the stairs.

What a good boy.

"Okay!" I released him.

He could not have made it up to the door faster. Once he was at the top, I clipped him into his leash, locked the door behind me, and unlatched the gate to exit our front backyard entrance.

Hoar frost coated the trees, making the winter wonderland look especially magnificent. We were nearing the edges of spring, with the day being slightly more temperate than I expected despite the frosty brush. There was still a light fog in the distance which added to the phenomena of the all-white, ice-covered world.

I took a right and headed down the street toward the greenstrip which was only a few blocks away. Riggley now walked beside me on the sidewalk. No. More. Pulling.

When we arrived at the off-leash I made a fist in front of me to ask Riggley to sit at the edge of the field. He sat without a verbal queue. I unclipped the leash and walked fifteen paces into the park, testing his stay.

He stayed.

"Okay!" I released him again like a shotgun.

My heart melted at his frolics as he ran in spontaneous paths through the entirety of the park, sniffing and marking everything. His black body and red raincoat, a stark contrast to the backdrop.

The ground wasn't covered in snow, just a light dusting of frost and a few patches last night's rain hadn't managed to soak through.

Each step I took through the field had a crisp texture under foot, like I was breaking the ice-coat on the grass with the pressure of my gait.

I walked directly to my favourite tree.

There were many trees in the park, but this one was at the edge of a clearing. When I came to this park at night it allowed me to have an open view of the moon and stars, and that's why I loved it so much. I often came here with Riggley when Jordan and I were at odds and I needed an escape, although I had also brought Jordan here with us when we would go for an evening walk.

I set down my backpack and reached for the blanket from within. I laid it out on the damp, slightly crunchy ground in front of the tree so that I could sit with my back against its trunk. I took out my crystal, lit the incense, and watched Riggley roam the park.

Jordan and I had been together for three years. The photo of our first unofficial Valentine's Day came to mind. We bonded deeply over our love for the same music and artists. He was older than I but by only a couple years.

Handsome, funny, caring, and kind, Jordan was the easiest person to talk to and kept a whip-smart, sarcastic sense of humor. At the start of our third year, we decided to move in together.

That's when things took a fateful turn. For some reason, the close proximity made both of us irritated with the other. I was particular about the dishwasher and wanted everything to have a home while he was all about the tetrisesque freestyle. He was particular about the laundry hamper and didn't appreciate the haphazard floorscapes I left strewn around the hamper but never inside it.

We both had trouble finding our flow as a pair.

In these last days, though, things had become tumultuous at best. This time, it was not about anything as trivial as laundry or dishes.

I ate Jordan's steak a month ago.

That may still sound trivial but the message it sent was rooted deeply in our dynamic and acted as a turning point for what came next.

Jordan enjoyed cooking good food—meats and veggies tastefully prepared with no sparing additional complexities. The only thing was that he often cooked well into the evening and sometimes in the early hours of the morning.

He had picked up two steaks from a butcher and marinated them for two days.

They were top quality with heavy marbling.

He made them with peppers stuffed with cream cheese and chives, and they were absolutely delicious. They were so big neither of us ate our whole steak.

Jordan then left for three days for work.

Thinking his leftovers were abandoned, I ate the one that was left behind as well as my own.

When Jordan returned, his attitude was abruptly snappy. His witty sarcasm was now cutting and aimed to sting. I didn't understand it at first, and I didn't clue in that it was due to my lack of consideration until he called it out a week later.

The awful realization that I was, in fact, inconsiderate lingered on me in a sordid way. I started believing the undertones in his words inferring I didn't care enough about him. I wasn't loving enough to be a good partner. I needed to do better.

Over the next few weeks, new arguments began to stir a frustration that I was always going to bed 'early'. Where 'early' was between an hour before or after midnight, which I considered 'quite late' even though I was trying to adjust to spend time with him.

This all climaxed the night before the Journey.

Jordan had asked me to stay up and go to bed with him. His reason was that he wanted to spend quality time together. I agreed, stipulating I didn't want to go to bed later than one o'clock, for if I allowed the agreement to be on his timeline, the sun could be coming up before he was ready for sleep.

Jordan spent the entire night watching hockey and ignoring me. If I tried to ask him a question, I would get a curt reply without any redirection of attention. It was like I wasn't there.

In the hour after midnight, I was doing my best to stay awake.

I got up and started attempting to train Riggley a new trick.

We had been working on 'Crawl' for a few days.

I would have Rigs lay down and stay then lay several treats in a line. I would then straddle him and keep his hips down as I released him to move forward to get the treats, telling him to 'Crawl'. If he made it to the last treat with his hips down, I would clap twice and tell him "Yesss!" then go fetch a piece of deli meat from the fridge.

This time, I had Riggley lay and stay, and I went and sat an arms width in front of him in the kitchen. I put a treat down right in front of me and said the verbal command "Crawl" while drawing a straight line from left to right with my right index finger to give him a hand signal, too.

The first few times he got up to retrieve his treat. I promptly took the treat away and had him return to 'Down' (flat hand moving down) and 'Stay' (flat hand moving forward like a 'stop' motion). I would then move back to my place and repeat the process.

Riggley seemed to be struggling with this a little. I could tell he was getting frustrated because every time I asked him to 'Crawl' he would get up faster and try to get to the treat before I took it away.

I concluded that we needed to go back a few steps before trying this one again.

I clapped my hands gently and let them fall to the side like a book telling Riggley "All Done!" to let him know that we were done training and he could relax his focus. Immediately Riggley came over to me and began attempting to give me kisses which I had to lean back and duck my head to escape.

I gave Rigs the treat in my hand so he didn't feel like I was withholding it from him.

Upon noticing that our training session was over, Jordan stopped the recaps that were now playing on the TV and came to sit with us in the kitchen.

Riggley settled and lay down at my feet so I could pet long strokes down his head and into the scruff of his neck.

"Glad you could pay attention to someone tonight." Jordan chose to start the conversation with a pointed remark.

"Someone was willing to receive it," I clapped back.

There was a pause.

I advocated for myself, speaking through the silence. "I tried to talk a few times tonight but you didn't seem interested."

"You must have read the room poorly. Sitting on the couch scrolling on your phone was not my idea of 'quality time'," he retorted.

"I don't think it's fair to put that all on me. You spent the evening watching your game. Same, same. No?" I was becoming annoyed. At least one of us had made efforts to connect.

"You're the best at avoiding taking accountability." Another snappy reply.

I looked at him with an icy gaze. "I am great at taking accountability when I deserve it."

Jordan returned eye contact with the same coldness he had received. "You never do."

Understanding that this wasn't an argument I was going to get out of unscathed, I gave Riggley a final pet and got up.

"I'm going to bed," I announced with a tone of irritation.

I left Jordan on the floor of the kitchen as I made the few paces down the hall to our tiny bathroom.

Rigs came and sat at the door to the bathroom as I began getting ready for bed. As I brushed my teeth, I reflected on my attitude.

My sass was not helping either of us, even if he was the one to dish it first. If I really wanted to be more patient, I should set the example.

I saw Riggley move before Jordan tried to enter the bathroom with me still inside.

"Just give me one moment," I asked him, mouth full of toothpaste, feeling suddenly cramped and claustrophobic with his husky frame behind me. I looked up into the mirror just in time to see him shake his head and walk away.

Another missed moment of connection.

I finished up in the bathroom and gave Riggley a head pet on my way to the bedroom. Knowing my routine, he passed me in the hall and led the way to the bed where he hopped up and settled into the spot he slept in between our feet.

Jordan must have gone back into the living room because he wasn't there.

I crawled into bed, leaving the light on in our closet as a dim sign that I was waiting for him. I got settled in the covers and Rigs let out a big huff of an exhale, letting me know he was tired, too.

I only had to wait a few minutes before I could hear Jordan getting ready in the bathroom and eventually making soft steps toward us.

I am Love

I reminded myself gently, bracing for the next round.

Jordan entered the bedroom. I rolled over into the centre of the bed to show that I was available.

Jordan went to the dresser and gathered a new shirt to change into. I watched him go through the motions of preparing for bed, including giving Riggley a kiss on the head and a few scritches before turning off the closet light and coming around to the side of the bed, getting in.

Away from me.

Ouch. I felt like a lot of what I did to show him I was present was in my body language. In the small gestures to be there. So often, this would be the return. A cold shoulder.

I laid there, wanting to reach out and touch his shoulder but fearing the rejection and sarcastic comment which might accompany it.

I stayed like that for several minutes, watching his silhouette rise and fall with every breath, wondering what was going through his mind.

Eventually, feeling defeated, I rolled over.

"So that's how it's going to be, hey?" I heard behind me.

I resisted the urge to snap back. I was offended I had shown availability and he hadn't. I don't know what silent signal I missed but I didn't feel like I was the one to blame for the entire interaction tonight.

"Jordan," I started softly, rolling back to the centre of the bed. "I don't know what you want me to do for you that I am not doing..."

My comment was honest and sincere. I was lost and unsure of how to rekindle the affection we used to show each other.

Jordan remained where he was. "You could start by initiating some form of connection."

I took a pause before replying. "I feel like every time I try I get shut down. I don't know how to break down your walls."

"Well, it feels like you're not trying at all." His response was quick.

A thousand thoughts ran through my head. Why was it always my job to remedy our issues? Why was it all on me to take accountability, apologize, bridge our episodes of silent treatment into communication? To communicate responsibly and with empathy?

Why was it always on me?

"Every time I try to connect, I feel like I get shut down, and every time I try to tell you the ways I am being present and making an effort to connect with you, I get called defensive."

"I don't do any of that. You just make up excuses to justify why you're always the one taking the higher ground."

Higher ground? Did he mean trying to talk to him like someone I wanted a longstanding relationship with?

I sat up in bed. "Jordan. I am trying. I am at a loss to know how to work together on this."

Jordan finally rolled up to look me in the eye. "Like you ever put 'together' into consideration since we've moved in. You've made this entire place into your own space, and you don't care that I only get a few days a week to spend together. It's like you're not excited to spend time with me."

I could feel my eyes pricking and my cheeks becoming flushed.

"I feel trapped. I can't even comment on that." My voice came out hitched.

"Try."

I paused to look in his eyes, trying to see if it was safe to proceed.

His expression was hard to read. His eyes were strained and I could see the hurt in them. I did my best to speak gently despite the rising turmoil. "I'm here all day, every day with Rigs. Of course it feels more like mine. I'm always here. Also, I want to connect with you. I really do. I just need you to give me a roadmap how."

Jordan rolled his eyes. "Maybe start by not eating my steak."

He rolled over with a huff.

I. Lost it.

Riggley's head shot up as I shot out of bed, not being able to tolerate the close proximity.

"Where are you going?"

I stormed to the edge of the door and looked back at him.

"If you can't accept the love I'm offering, I don't know what more I can do!" The words came out violently as I exited the room, slamming the door shut behind me.

In the park, Riggley had finished his circuit through the clearing and was now laying on the grass beside me.

I looked at the park in front of me. The sun cast shadows through the branches of my tree onto the ground. A warm wind gently rustled my hair. A drop of melt landed on my shoulder.

I took a deep breath, shifting from my reverie to the beautiful day before me.

I took my journal out of my backpack and went through the pack to find my pen.

Found it.

I sat with pen hovering over paper. In the past year, I had developed a penchant for poetry. I would write scribbles in my journal, hoping to articulate the feelings I was experiencing. I focused on the sensations of last night.

I closed my eyes and let the words surface from their depths within my soul.

The words arrived as the message of my Shamanic Journey had. My mind was quiet in one breath, and in the next, words sang themselves in a chord near silence. I had to be still to hear them.

> *A connection crushed*
> *A union shushed*
> *Be light my spirit*
> *Be still and hear it*

Sometimes I was embarrassed by how bland the words could be, but I transcribed them into my journal anyway. I liked the experience of listening for words which could hardly be heard.

I suddenly felt a surge of emotion as I read the words over. I wiped tears from my face and looked up at the sky.

Why?

I asked the question and expected the cosmos to give me a response. I listened closely. I held my pen over paper, hearing nothing.

Of course not. Speaking to The Universe occurred in subtle ways. Ritual helped to facilitate the conversation, but I never received a clear answer. Only whiffs and hints of what I needed to pay attention to.

I stretched, raising my hands above my head. I had spent enough time in reflection, and the chill of last night's freezing rain still lingered despite the chinook's warming breeze.

Folding my blanket as Riggley took a few last sniffs, I gathered up my journal and other items and returned them to the backpack.

"Ready to go?" I asked.

Riggley's tail wagged.

We walked over to the edge of the park, with Rigs a few strides ahead of me.

When we reached the edge of the park, I called him back to me and got him to sit again before clipping the leash back to his collar.

From there, we walked back through frosty, slowly melting streets to the house.

Considering the mystical nature of my Shamanic Journey, for the very first time in my life I considered going to see a psychic.

I had known of psychics from stories of shady entrances where one might walk through a beaded curtain into a small room with a small table and a large crystal ball. I imagined heavy incense and a heavily adorned woman taking my naivety as easily as my money and leaving me with pipe dreams and a road to ruin.

There was a psychic at a metaphysical shop in town. I had gone into the store multiple times to look at their crystals and books and always paused at the sign offering their services.

Riggley and I returned to the house, stopping to sniff out the backyard on our way back.

Once he made his way to the door, I opened it and called him inside.

"Paws!" I told Rigs as he passed the doorway and took a step down the stairs.

I had a towel at the top of the stairs to clean his feet during the winter months when his paws arrived home coated in filth from our adventures.

Riggley waited patiently on the top of the landing as I had him lift each paw by tapping his shoulder or hind leg to let him know which one I wanted him to raise for me. I cleaned each paw, ensuring I wiped between the toe beans before I removed his raincoat and asked him to sit..

I descended the stairs, and once I was at the bottom, told Rigs, "Okay!"

He raced down and made himself comfortable in his crate, located in the living room between the table and sofa.

I deliberately ignored my dog as I discarded his leash and coat and then walked out of the house with the jacket and backpack still on my shoulders.

I heard him whine as I closed the door, but it was a necessary process in reducing his anxiety when we left.

My car was coated in frost. I opened the door to turn the vehicle on and start the defrosting process as I collected my brush from the floor of the passenger seat.

I closed the door behind me to keep in any heat and started scraping the windows.

It took me two or three minutes to scrape and brush. When I was done and back in the vehicle, it seemed to be slightly warmer than before.

For a few minutes I sat, idling, ensuring the engine had time to warm up before I shifted into reverse and pulled out of the parking spot.

I navigated myself easily to the metaphysical shop in a trendy hipster neighbourhood where it was often hard to find parking. I parked several blocks away and walked, soaking the toes of my shoes in the mushy meltage forming on the sidewalks and street corners.

As I opened the door, a man standing behind the till greeted me. "Hello! Can we help you today?"

"Hi there!" I replied. "I'm looking into getting a reading. Do you have any more information?"

"I do." The guy came out from around the till to speak with me. His ears were pierced with large, round disks and he had a huge, fluffy afro dyed deep blue at the tips. He wore natural-looking material beneath an apron which appeared to be part of the shop's uniform. "Our readers are by appointment only and they are all booked today, but I can give you more details in case you'd like to come back?"

I should have known better than to think I could just walk in. "That would be great."

The man held a friendly demeanour and told me the logistics, how long the sessions were, and how much they cost. Shocked at the expense, I smiled at him and asked if he had ever gotten a reading.

"I have, and it was incredible. It told me everything I needed to know and more."

He asked if I wanted to book an appointment and I declined. "I'll call back if I change my mind."

The shop was full of crystals, gemstones, and books. I always got caught in the books. There were so many of them that I could never decide which one to pick up and turn over in my hands. My fingertips brushed over the spines, and I took in a deep breath.

The books on the shelves of this store were all spiritual in nature. There were several texts about crystals and the healing properties of them. Some of the books were about philosophies on life and how to live in an enlightened way. I had a few of the popular ones of both.

I decided that I didn't need another book today, however, after the Shamanic Journey, I did want some herbs. I loved the experience of smoke cleansing and wanted to start to involve it in my practice. The shelf where they stored the dried herb was a few steps away. They had bundles and loose sage, cedar, mugwort, juniper, and palo santo. I chose a bundle of each cedar and mugwort and a small, spiralled shell.

I paid for my purchases and walked back to my car.

I was still unsure of my interest in getting a reading. On one hand, more clarity on the message of my Shamanic Journey felt like it would be beneficial. On the other, I was afraid of what it would say. I wasn't ready, but perhaps there was someone I could consult who could help me feel more at ease.

Intro to Tarot

> Hey Nicole! Are you free?

I sent my best friend a text from the back parking spot when I arrived back at the house.

The message of my Journey had been *You, alone.* Pratibha Yoga Festival. I wondered if Nicole had any insight. She was accompanying me to the festival, after all.

Riggley stayed at the bottom landing as I opened the door.

"Sit," I told him before descending the stairs.

He licked my fingers, asking for pets as I walked to the kitchen.

I put my adventure pack back in the bedroom closet and ignored him. He followed close behind me as I moved to the kitchen.

Withholding affection from him was uncomfortable, but it really had been helping him stay calmer when we were gone. I was no longer finding our clothes pulled into his crate or hearing him howling from the parking spot as I got back home.

As I was settling down on the dark grey chaise sofa under the only window in the room, Riggley came to lay at my feet. I gave him a few minutes of calm while scrolling Social Media on my phone before reaching down to run a few strokes on his soft ears. He lifted his head and licked at my hands. For a moment, I let him.

My phone made a sharp pinging sound, notifying me that I had an incoming message. I brought my hand back up to my phone.

> Yes! What's up, Hun? I'm off today.

Riggley put his head down on his paws as I texted my reply.

> Would you come over? I need to talk to someone.

I noted that I had yet to eat breakfast. It only took a few steps for me to reach the fridge and look again at my limited options.

I took a spoon out of our white veneer drawers which were found below our grey laminate countertops that lined the wall adjacent to the spare room. I started mixing a cup of yogurt with some granola I found in our white veneer pantry cabinets when my phone made another notification tone.

> On my way!

She didn't live far and would be here in a few minutes. I sat down on the tile floor of the kitchen, right before the flooring transitioned to the soft grey carpet of the living room and began to eat my breakfast. Our high-top, dark wood, square table was not beloved to me. It didn't fit the space in the slightest. It was one of Jordan's contributions to the house, and I desperately wanted to switch it out but was afraid of further comments of my influence on the space.

I finished my yogurt and granola and noted that the dishwasher was full. I put the cup in the sink and filled it with water to soak, then popped a detergent pod into the dishwasher to run it. The moment I pressed the start button, the doorbell rang.

Riggley sat up and started to howl.

I hurried down the hallway to the door with Rigs following.

"Just a second!" I called, trying to get Riggley into a 'Sit'.

He was not listening and kept barking at the door.

I would typically handle this with patience but the only way to accomplish that was to ask Nicole to wait at the door for upwards of ten minutes as he calmed down.

The pressure of prioritization in conjunction with the chaos of Riggley barking overwhelmed me.

Nicole knocked on the door again to which Riggley began trying to get around me and up the stairs. I pushed back at him and took him by the collar, leading him into the bedroom where I closed the door.

The regression of this would affect us later.

I ran up the stairs and opened the door to see my best friend with a bag full of chocolate smiling at me.

"Hey, Love! Come on in!" I opened the door wider.

Nicole was a beautiful girl. Her eyes were her most attractive feature. They were an icy, piercing blue with a friendly constriction at the corners. We were contrasts to each other with our height differences. My bright blonde, shoulder-length waves ended where her deep purple, waist-length hair began. The side of her head was shaved short, and a mandala flower was 'tattooed' into her hair.

She had been my best friend for years, our bond growing over our evolving spirituality. Nicole has been an unwavering cheerleader as I built myself into the person I am today. She kept pace with me in my pursuits to be a better version of myself, not once taking the ways I'd course-corrected and seen a stranger.

"Is Riggley not getting better?" she asked as I led her down the stairs and took her coat to hang it up in the hall closet.

"He's getting better with me, but the doorbell is a whole other ordeal," I told her as Riggley's muffled barks came from our bedroom. "Are you ready for me to let him out?"

I wanted to release him before he started chewing the doorknob.

"Go for it! Poor guy." Nicole was empathetic to our struggles and likely would have waited until he was ready if I had asked.

"This is going to be hard, but please just ignore him a little until he's calm," I asked her as I opened the door to the bedroom.

Riggley charged out, barking and whining, his tail doubling down on the wags so much that his whole slender body was rippling with motion stemming from his hips.

Nicole understood my request and did not engage, though he licked at her hands asking for a greeting.

"This way." I led Nicole to the living room with Riggley in tow.

As we sat down on the sofa, Nicole leaned over to give me a warm hug.

"What's on your mind, Hun?" she asked sincerely. "You seem stressed."

With Rigs still at the edge of the sofa asking for attention, I started to unravel. I told her all about the Shamanic Journey. "I don't know what to do about this, Nic! My mind sincerely doubts that leaving Jordan is the right decision, even though I know in my heart I can't keep doing this."

She looked at me for a little while. "Well, I think you need to figure it out. I know this is going to take some time, but it's really weighing on you."

I sighed, popping a chocolate into my mouth and chewing softly.

"I know. I wish I didn't have to make the decision myself and someone would just tell me what to do. I almost booked a session with a psychic for guidance," I said with a half-hearted laugh.

"I've never seen a psychic, but I know a woman who does similar readings. She's a medium and pretty intuitive. Her name is Tony, and she leads the Red Tent Circles I go to." Nicole also slipped a chocolate out of the bag separating us on the couch.

"I don't actually know if I want to see someone about it. I was just curious." I looked at her.

"Well, I have a tarot deck now because of her. I actually brought it today just in case! Want to see if we can get some answers?" she asked.

"When did you get a tarot deck?"

"After Tony gave me an oracle deck! I guess the rule is that a deck has to be gifted to you before you can buy one... I just picked up this deck of tarot cards yesterday," she explained. I was amazed at the timing.

"Okay, I want to try it with you. It didn't feel right when I looked into it at the metaphysical shop."

"I've never actually done a reading, but it will be fun to try it out, and it might give some answers to what you've been struggling with."

Nicole shifted off the couch onto the floor to sit at the edge of my coffee table. The art print of a gorilla smoking a fat doobie with rainbow eyeglasses fixed above the couch acted as a comical frame to the weight of what I was dealing with.

Riggley had calmed down and was lying on the floor but immediately got up to give Nicole kisses as she sat down.

"May I?" she asked.

I laughed. "Yes, he's good now."

Nicole giggled as she petted Rigs and attempted to avoid his wet nose.

I got up to retrieve the cedar from my bag of purchases I left on the counter and a lighter from the drawer before returning to sit across from Nicole. We made the black wooden coffee table into an altar and lit the cedar bundle to cleanse ourselves with the smoke.

Rigs had settled again and was lying calmly beside Nicole as she gave him sweet pets between his ears.

Nicole suggested saying a mantra. "I know the mantra of Ganesh! Ganesh is the elephant deity who is known to be the remover of obstacles."

"I think it's the perfect one." I shifted my seat so that I was in a more comfortable sitting position. Nicole took her tarot deck out of her bag. The deck was thicker than the average card game variety and the cards themselves were taller, too. The cards were all printed with blue and purple swirls on the back face. The colours combined like eddies of a current, folding and weaving through each shade.

Nicole held them gently in her hands before pulling out her phone and finding the mantra to show me.

I took her phone, then together we chanted the words of the mantra on her screen as she shuffled.

"*Ohm, Gam Ganapataye Namaha.*"

She traded me the deck for her device.

"Settle into stillness. Get clear, ask your question, cut the deck, and then we'll pull some cards," Nicole told me.

I sat in front of her and closed my eyes. I waited until I felt still and then asked:

What is the root of this conflict with Jordan? How do I move forward?

I cut the deck at the upper third. Nicole took the cards back from me and pulled four cards, setting them down on the surface of the coffee table in a line.

"In this spread the cards are supposed to represent the situation, obstacle, action, and outcome," she explained, her hand brushing each card in its respective position.

She looked up at me. "Are you ready?"

We held eye contact for a moment before I nodded.

She flipped the cards so that we could see their faces.

The first card was backwards to Nicole and upright to me.

It depicted a tree with a sturdy trunk blooming into a crown of green leaves. There were coins interspersed throughout this headpiece made of foliage. The branches were spindly and reaching.

The remaining cards were upright to Nicole.

The second card was a light purple and depicted a girl wearing a long dress caught in the wind. She was blindfolded and surrounded by swords. The sky above her, streaked with lightning.

The third card was a single golden coin which took up the majority of the face. It had branches weaving through its facets, dripping like a weeping willow tree from its base. The backdrop of the card was deep green, a forest with muted details.

Lastly, the final card was the brightest of yellows. With a sun on its face, wispy strands of shining light emanated from the glowing orb. Swirls within the sun made it appear to be smiling.

All cards were bordered in black, with extra space for their title written in white ink at the bottom.

I was confused about the first card which appeared upside down. "What does that mean?" I asked.

"I think when they're upside down it means the opposite of when they're right side up. It's called a reversal. Why don't we look at the book and see what we can interpret?"

Nicole began to flip through the guidebook and read aloud the meaning of each of the cards.

The Situation: KING OF PENTACLES [REVERSED]
Stuck in a rut.
Fearing commitment due to possessiveness.

The Obstacle: EIGHT OF SWORDS
Intellectual imprisonment.
There is a way out but you cannot see it.

The Action: ACE OF PENTACLES
New enterprises.
Introducing something new will bring you abundance.

The Outcome: THE SUN
Optimism.
Things are going to get a lot better!
It's all going to be okay.

As soon as Nicole read the meanings from the guidebook, the words felt like truth. Her interpretation felt like everything I already knew.

I felt Jordan had been asking *me* to be the source of his happiness instead of looking for it himself.

My beliefs on relationships stated that two people should be responsible for their own happiness while doing their best to maintain it in the company of each other. I believed that each person had to manifest their happiness themselves but should be supported in this pursuit by their partner.

Jordan seemed to think happiness is found in the other person and the purpose of a relationship is to 'complete' ourselves. He sought for me to 'complete' him.

This difference elicited a constant source of tension between the two of us. I wasn't ready to commit to him until he stopped trying to control the way I showed him love.

"I just wish Jordan and I could reconcile our differences. We've been stuck in the same cycle for months." I looked up at Nicole, sparing her the details.

"I wonder if there is something you could do to make him see how hard you're trying to figure this out, but also to gently let him know that something needs to shift for you to stay." Nicole took my hand and squeezed it.

I tapped the second card.

The Eight of Swords. I picked it up and turned it over. The obstacle.

"The message of the Journey was 'You, alone'. I'm not sure there is a way out of this which doesn't involve breaking up... I've told Jordan so many times I feel like a bird trapped in a cage. I don't know what I can do to keep us together." I sniffed, wiping a delicate trail of moisture from my bottom lashes with the back of my hand still holding the card.

Nicole squeezed again. "We'll find something if that's what you want."

"I don't want to lose him..." I trailed.

For a moment we were silent. Riggley's heavy breathing was the only noise to break the silence.

"I really like this card." I put the Eight of Swords down.

"Me too. I really like this deck. I think it suits me." She reached into her bag. "Here."

I looked at her hands. She was offering me a different deck of cards. "Here is the oracle deck that I got. It's a gift to you so you can get a deck, too!"

I took the cards from Nicole's hands. 'Native American Oracle' was written in golden foil on the front with a dreamcatcher set against a wooden textured backdrop.

"Thank you, Lovely." I cooed. "Are you sure?"

"Yes, I'm sure. You're the one who wants to expand her spiritual practice! It's time to get a deck."

"Okay, okay" I laughed. "So what do I do now?"

"New enterprises! What do you think that could mean?"

I pondered the thought for a moment.

The cards didn't quite tell me what to do, but they did reflect how I was feeling. I craved an outlet to start fresh, utilize my creativity, and find myself.

"Well, I just know that it has something to do with intuition, and spirituality." A whiff of memory from the Journey came to mind. I popped another chocolate into my mouth and spoke around it. "I'd like to create something!"

"Oh! What would you like to create?"

"I'm not sure, but I felt strongly in the part of my Journey where the women were in the red room that there was something I was meant to share." I felt inspired.

"That's neat! I'm sure anything you made would be helpful for others." Nicole smiled encouragingly.

"I wonder if something will happen at the Yoga Festival!" I mused.

"I wondered that, too. Who knows, maybe something will happen there that will lead you forward!"

The card spread in front of me was perplexing. I didn't understand how it could be so accurate.

The Sun. Everything was going to be okay.

I relaxed. The cards answered my questions perfectly. They didn't tell me what to do about separating from Jordan, but they did imply that there was more waiting for me beyond the relationship.

"Thank you for the reading." I looked up at Nicole.

She smiled at me. "You're welcome! I hope it helped."

I held the gifted deck in my hands and felt a pull toward them.

If chose to lean in... where could these new enterprises lead me?

Two Little Things

Nicole stayed for a while longer before leaving to go run her own errands for the afternoon. I gave her a big hug as she left the house, thanking her for coming over.

I leaned against the back of the closed door, processing, not moving. It was impossible to believe that I had investigated psychics for the first time today and instead received a tarot reading in a sacred and special way. Gratitude and curiosity overwhelmed me. I was still so new to New Age spirituality; I had known of some of the intuitive services the community provided but had always been skeptical of them. Now, disbelief in how accurate the reading had been struck me. I wondered how it all worked...

I knew one thing for sure: this experience had just fuelled my desire to dive deeper into this world. I was excited.

Finally, I moved away from the door and back to the couch where Nicole and I sat for my reading. The cedar was still sitting on the coffee table beside the Native American Oracle deck Nicole had gifted me.

I started to clear both away and take them and my other purchases to the bedroom where I stored my spiritual paraphernalia in a small box hidden under the bed. Something vulnerable within me felt like protecting this part of myself from Jordan. I didn't want to allow a chance for him to make a snappy comment about the crystals I had been collecting, the journal I scribbled poetry in, or the slender white intention candle that I liked to burn when I meditated in ritual.

As I opened the box, a heat rose to my face.

I wanted to practice my spirituality openly. I wanted to be *me*.

The yoga. The meditation. The search for answers and wisdom within the visions of the Shamanic Journey.

I didn't want to hide any longer.

Jordan and I had signed a lease for the year in the summer and we would be up to re-sign it in just a few months.

When we moved into the space, we piled our moving boxes into the spare room and used the space as a hub to unpack from. Somewhere along the way we stopped unpacking, deciding that our extra things were not as valuable as we once thought. The room was a mess, and we usually kept the door closed.

With resolve, I walked down the hall, stopping at the door. Riggley came to meet me from his crate in the dining room.

I opened the door and stood in the doorway.

There weren't many boxes, and scattered on the floor were just the odds and ends that didn't yet have homes. I walked into the centre of the room and sat down on the floor, starting to consolidate the items within my own boxes—piles to keep, to sort, and to throw away formed on the floor.

Riggley made his way into the room and lay down in the corner clear of mess.

It took me the better part of an hour to sort through my share of the belongings, and when I was done, I looked toward Jordan's. It felt weird to go through his things, so I opted to tidy up the loose ends on the floor into one of the boxes I had emptied. I needed to get creative with the closet, but eventually managed to stack up all the boxes that were left and shut the closet doors.

An empty room.

Finally.

With the room clear and free of debris, Riggley came to my side and licked my hands. I made my way to the floor so I could hug his scruff. The licks migrated to my ears, making me giggle and laugh.

During my organization, I found some twinkly white christmas lights and pictures of Jordan and I when we first started dating.

I walked back to my bedroom and brought out my little box from under the bed, then stole the coffee table from the living room to create an altar. I strung lights on the surface and arranged crystals and trinkets on the coffee table. I placed the white candle in the centre with my quartz crystal in front of it. I set the burned end of the cedar bundle into my new spiralled shell to the right, protecting the table from soot. The cedar still smelled like a forest but a whiff of the charred, smoky scent lingered now that it had been used. I propped my favourite photo up at the back of the table.

My box of spiritual things, now only containing the oracle deck, was tucked away on the floor. I collected my journal and my yoga mat from the bedroom and laid them in front of the table. When everything finally had a place, my final task was to grab a cushion off the couch and sit on it in the middle of my mat, facing my altar.

I beamed.

Finally.

The ambiance of the room was cozy with the soft glow of the twinkly lights. I was about to light the candle when a knock at the door disturbed the motion.

Riggley jolted from his spot beside me and howled as he rushed out of the room to the adjacent stairs to meet the intruder.

The faint sound of laughter from outside had me abandon my meditation and get up to greet my favourite souls.

The window to the spare room was just outside the door to our suite. I opened it and whispered, "Pssst!"

"HALLIE!" Little voices screeched my name.

Riggley returned to my side to investigate the commotion.

"Hi, Brook. Hi, Fable," I murmured through the fly screen. "To what do I owe this surprise?"

"To what? A surprise?" The older of the two, Fable, appeared confused.

I laughed. "It's a phrase. I'm asking why you are knocking on my door."

"OH! We came to see if you and Riggley wanted to go for a walk!" she said, her sister watching Riggley behind me and absentmindedly playing with her mittens.

"I already went for a walk today, but I suppose I could go for another." I assessed the two of them and deemed them to both be prepared with gloves, hats, coats, and only slightly rosy cheeks.

"Can you wait for me to open the door?" I asked. "It's locked, but I'll be there in just a moment!"

Fable nodded. "We'll wait."

Riggley was at my heels and excited.

I grabbed his leash from the closet and put it into my coat pocket.

Standing at the base of the stairs, I took a brief moment to train door behaviour. "Sit."

Riggley sat. His tail was wagging, but he sat.

"Stay." I paused to ensure the command before walking up the stairs.

Riggley stayed as I went up.

I put on my boots quickly before I unlocked and opened the door a crack. He lifted his hips.

"Sit."

Hips returned to the tile.

I opened the door.

Riggley stayed in a seat as I stepped outside.

The daylight was dull and fading at this time of day, yet I still had to squint at the brightness. A slight chill brushed my face, but it was nothing like the damp freeze of last night.

I looked back to find Rigs in the same place, feeling proud, I told him, "Okay!"

The clomping of feet immediately preceded Riggley running out the door and down the stairs of the small landing. He greeted the girls who giggled and laughed as he licked their faces, checking for treats of snack time left behind.

"Riggley!" I called, attempting to deter and redirect the behaviour.

He came back to the landing, and I gave him scruff scruffs.

"What day is it today?" Brook was looking at me intently, still standing beside the window. On her third solar return, her face was round under messy raven-black hair, the top of which captured strands in a loose ponytail to keep it (mostly) off her face. Her dark brown eyes were fixed on mine as she dropped down into a crouch and picked up a crunchy ball of brown, frost-coated grass from the walkway. "Is it Christmas?"

"Hunnie, we already had Christmas! Today is the first Saturday of March," I told her as I let go of Rigs, who left my side to explore the backyard.

"Christmas is in December," Fable told her year-younger sister in a small but knowing voice. She played with her dark blonde braid which curled tightly into coils after the tie, looping the coils in her fingers. "We have a loooong way to go before it's December again."

I took a few steps down from the landing to meet them by the window and the gate.

"I can understand how you think it's Christmas, though! It's so white and wonderland-like out here today!" I crouched down and extended my arms to Brook who slowly dropped her dirt cluster and came to embrace me in a hug.

Fable came to my side, and I raised an arm to include her, balancing precariously on my toes.

"You said you wanted to go for a walk?" I asked.

"Yes!" Fable exclaimed.

"Can we go see your mom first?"

"Yeah, she's baking right now." Fable let me go.

Understanding the assignment, I decided to keep it quick.

"Okay, let's go!"

I detached from Brook and unlatched the front gate, ushering them out and closing it on Riggley so he wasn't barging in with us. I planned to collect him shortly.

As the gate closed, Rigs barked once to remind us he was left behind.

"Be right back, Buddy," I told him.

We rounded the corner to the stairs leading to the upper suite. I let the girls lead me into their home, instantly being greeted by a rush of warm air and the rich smell of baking chocolate.

"Heyy!" Danielle called across the half-counter separating their kitchen from the entryway. She was a generation older than I was, with pepper and plum hair and the kindest blue eyes.

The girls kept their boots on and crowded, discussing what they got from Santa this year, in the entry.

"How long do you need?" Our casual and established relationship allowed me to get straight to the point.

"Like, twenty minutes." Her hands were sticky with cupcake mixture. "Bake sale. They can frost a few when you get back!"

"Got it." I nodded, my hands meeting Fable's back, herding her back toward the door. "Come on, girls."

"Yay! Can we go to the playground?" Fable asked.

"That sounds like a great idea!" I told her as we walked down their front steps.

As I rounded the corner, Riggley was still waiting at the gate.

I pulled the leash out of my coat pocket and opened the gate to collect him.

He sniffed the girls faces again but stayed close enough that I could clip him in.

"Let's go!" I announced. The little feet skipped and jumped ahead to round the house and head west down the sidewalk. They knew the way.

"Do you remember the rules?" I asked.

"Don't cross the street without you. Wait at the corner," Fable said in monotone.

"You got it!"

Brook ran three steps ahead and then looked back at me.

"Do you want to hold my hand?" I asked, offering the hand that wasn't holding Rigs' leash.

She nodded and as I caught up, her gentle, somehow already wet mitten enclosed on my bare hand.

Fable leaped ahead until she reached the street corner. She turned around to look at the distance between us. "You guys should hurrrrrrry!"

"Fable, how high can you jump?" I asked her.

She tried twice. "This high!"

By the time she landed her second jump, we had caught up. "Wow! That's amazing. Can you look both ways? Is it clear to cross?"

Both girls looked in either direction.

"It's clear," Fable said, nodding.

"Then let's cross."

The playground was two blocks away from home. Brook let go of my hand the moment sidewalk turned to grass and bolted for the equipment.

Rigs and I kept nearby, watching for missed steps as the girls climbed and ran, and occasionally playing "I'm gonna get you!" with their feet where I could reach them. They would squeal and run through the equipment claiming, "No you're not!"

I kept watch on their cheeks and noses, trying to determine when the brisk chill of the near evening was going to sour their happy attitudes.

After the designated twenty minutes had been reached and my own fingers were red and stiff, I called to the girls, "Do you want to decorate cupcakes now?"

Fable was quick to get off the playground and come running to my side. Rigs gave her pink cheek a quick greeting lick. Brook was sitting on the top of the slide, unmoving.

"Brook!" I said, walking over. "Want to go down the slide again?"

She shook her head.

"Do you want down another way?" I asked.

She shook her head.

This was a trap, and I knew it.

"Hunnie, it's time to go home. We can come back again," I reasoned.

Tears.

"I don't... I don't... I don't," was all she could get out.

"Brook doesn't want to go!" Fable filled in the blanks.

"I know, Hunnie," I spoke directly to Brook. "Do you see the sun? How it's getting lower? Soon it's going to be dark, and it gets a little scary when it's dark at the park. We need to get home safe before then."

I couldn't reach Brook from the bottom of the slide. It would have to be her choice because if I went up there, history would say that a full tantrum would begin.

I chose to employ a tactic that I had been using with Rigs at the door. Extinction.

With Riggley, I had sat a few steps away from top of the stairs and had him lay down at the bottom.

I would practice standing, and if he stood too, I would sit down.

He would look at me, confused, but eventually sit again, and if I waited long enough, he would lay down.

I would give him a minute before I tried to stand again.

If I could rise and move upward a step without him standing, I would throw a few treats down the stairs to confirm the correct response.

I did this for several long hours, across different evenings when Jordan wasn't home. I contributed this training to his exponential improvement.

Brook wasn't a dog, obviously. However, I was learning that patience was an incredibly effective tool.

"Okay, Hunnie. We're going to sit here and wait for you to come down. When you're ready to come home, go down the slide." I sat cross-legged at the base of the slide, just to the right of its exit-path. Rigs lay down beside me.

I pulled Fable into my lap and whispered in her ear, "This could take a little bit. Let's be still and listen to the trees."

Brook now had only one way out. If she returned down the equipment, I would be able to get her easily and was prepared for the cries and deadweight that would follow if I chose to pick her up.

The path of least resistance was down the slide.

I let the breeze sweep Fable's wispy wayward strands of hair into my face, the gentle tickle a minor distraction as I pretended I wasn't waiting for Brook.

We sat for a minute or two in silence with only the sounds of the street to accompany us. The occasional passing car across the park. Other kids playing at the ball pitches further on. Birds chirping in the trees.

Eventually, feeling into the moment and sensing that Brook had softened, I asked her again. "Are we ready for some cupcakes?"

I extended my arms, as through to invite her onto my lap also. Her face seemed hesitant, but with a little shuffle she was suddenly sliding down to us.

Fable and I laughed as we ducked away from the slide, both spilling into the wet gravel.

I got up and offered Fable my hand to right her. Once she was up, I turned to Brook.

Riggley was at her side, and she was holding on to his collar to steady herself.

"Good job, Hunnie!" I told her. "Would you like a piggyback home?"

She nodded, to my relief. I hoped that making the way home a novel mode of transport would prevent further resistance.

I still didn't trust Riggley not to tow Fable, so I kept hold of the leash as I crouched down to let Brook climb onto my back.

She vice gripped her hands together around my collar bones and squished her knees around my hips.

I hooked her calves under my forearms and started heading back to the house with Riggley and Fable beside me.

Fable didn't have the same excitement as she did on our way there and instead, she talked to me about her upcoming bake sale.

"It's for our school. We need to bake four dozen treats!" she said.

"Do you know how many that is?" I asked, testing her vocabulary.

"Mom says a dozen is twelve. I don't know how many four twelves is, exactly, but I know it's four trays of cupcake tins!" Her brightness constantly impressed me.

"Four twelves is a lot to bake! We can count them all when we're done!"

We crossed the street together, Brook silently enjoying her ride home.

"What colour of icing do you think we'll put on the cupcakes?" I asked Fable.

"Blue!"

"Purple!"

I couldn't tell which colour came from which voice as they were exclaimed at the same time, but I expected no different answers than the ones I received.

"Blue and Purple, hey? I'm sure we can put in a special request." We had rounded the corner of the house and Brook started to squirm.

"Do you want down?" I asked.

More squirms and a soft whimpery grunt confirmed her intentions. I bent my knees and lowered so that Brook could dismount.

The two of them ran from me across the front lawn up to the steps of their door.

"CUPCAKES!"

They announced their arrival home as I followed them, taking a short detour to secure Riggley in the backyard.

"Be right back, go explore!" I told him, hoping he would settle after a walk.

He whined as I closed the gate, but his tail was neutral and he didn't appear too anxious.

I left him to go support what I'm sure was moderate chaos upstairs.

As I opened the door and walked into the entry, the girls were in their living room to the left. I peeked around the corner to see them bouncing on the couch cushions.

My eyebrows tilted up at the abundance of energy they were expressing.

"Thank you," Dani said behind me. "Do you want to stay around to help frost?"

"Of course!" I moved to the kitchen to see that there were two trays of vanilla cupcakes steaming on the counter beside two cooling racks of chocolate.

"Let's let them play a little before they realize they're missing out." Danielle had a piping bag full of purple icing in her hand, fixing it with a flower tip.

I took the bag from her and got to work on one of the chocolate cupcakes as screams and giggles emanated from the front room.

"Are things going better with Riggley?" Dani asked as she started mixing blue colouring into a bowl of icing. "I haven't heard him at the door as much."

"He's doing so, so much better," I confirmed. "Thank you again. You and Phillip were lifesavers for a while there."

At the beginning of our time in this rental, any time Riggley was left at home, whether it was a quick run to the grocery store or an evening where Jordan and I tried to spend out by ourselves or with friends, Rigs had yelped and whined at the door. Considering that there was a permanently locked door connecting Dani's kitchen to the top of our stairs with a little gap at the bottom, it had been quite the disturbance on the family.

Instead of complaining or making a fuss, Danielle had sent me a message on a particularly challenging night asking for the code to our door. She brought him into their house so he wasn't alone, and this small gesture was the initiation of a depth of friendship I never expected to gain.

"That's amazing. It's not a problem. I'm glad he's been more relaxed at home. He's lucky to have a momma like you!" The icing appeared well-mixed and quite blue.

I had been putting in a lot of effort to help Riggley, and appreciated the praise.

"How has it been with Jordan?" she asked gently.

I had yet to confide in her about our challenges and the question caught me off guard.

"Things are fine," I lied as I focused on my swirl technique.

"I heard you raise your voice the other night." She stopped her transfer of icing into piping bag and came to lean against the counter beside me. "I don't think that comes naturally to you."

My eyes pricked and my breathing constricted.

I wanted to save his reputation with them, even though he hadn't been earning it himself.

"I don't want you to think differently of him," I confided.

"Hallie, we care about *you*," Danielle emphasized. "I just want to make sure you're okay."

I nodded as I continued to concentrate on the task of creating perfect loops with the icing. "I'll be okay. We're just struggling to find our flow."

"Well, we're here if you need it. You know you can crash on the couch if you need a safe space, even if it's in the middle of the night." Her care meant so much to me.

I looked up to meet her gentle ocean gaze. "Thank you, hopefully I won't."

The sound of the door opening diverted my attention.

"Smells like a snack in here!"

Phillip had his hands full with a lunch bag, a satchel, and was dirty, dirty, dirty.

"You stay away from the kitchen! These are not for snacking." Danielle gave him a serious look.

"Your boyfriend is home." Phillip looked at me. "Does he know how to say 'hello'?"

My heart became weighted as the door to our suite could be heard opening through the gap and the patter of paws sounded as Riggley must have descended the stairs.

I froze. Jordan wasn't supposed to be home until tomorrow! Also, the door to the spare room was open. There was no way that Jordan wouldn't see what I had done.

Once it sounded like Jordan had cleared the entry, I turned to Phillip and asked under breath, "again?"

Despite Danielle and Phillip being kind enough to care for his dog for us, Jordan could not be bothered to acknowledge them.

"Again," Phillip confirmed in a casual voice.

It made me sad to know that I had such a wonderful relationship with my neighbours and Jordan didn't want to participate in it at all. He was so cold to them when all they had done was show warmth.

"I'm sorry. I don't know why he's being like that. I don't understand it either," I confided.

Phillip shrugged. "So, do you have any insurance?"

Puzzled, I frowned. "Insurance?"

"Insurance! So I don't eat all those cupcakes."

Danielle rolled her eyes. "I need to make these for the girls first. It's been a long day! You can go get ice cream. They'll be out of the house tomorrow morning."

"Girls! Ice Cream!" he called.

"ICE CREAM!!" I heard in tandem accompanied by a stampede of tiny feet.

"You'll take them?" I asked.

"Yeh. Unless you want to come?" Phillip moved past the kitchen and headed toward the bedrooms at the back of the suite.

"I'm helping your wife," I called, knowing they weren't legally married. "Have fun!"

There was a fast-food place a few blocks away from us which served ice cream I assumed he would be walking to with the girls.

"Want me to take your dog?" I heard through a closed door.

I didn't want to yell, so I focused on my next cupcake, one of the last of a dozen.

The girls were in the kitchen now, asking when their dad was taking them.

"Soon, Hunnies. Do you want to watch?" I asked.

Fable nodded as Brook tugged on her mom's apron.

"Come here," I said to Fable as I led her around the kitchen counter to the entry. She followed, and I lifted her from the back of the counter to sit on the raised ledge. "Don't let your feet get into the cupcakes."

I was about to turn back into the kitchen when Brook appeared at my side. "Do you want up, too?"

A nod. A hoist. Two girls on the ledge.

"Don't lean back too far, and keep your feet out of the cupcakes," I repeated.

I moved to return to the other side of the counter. The girls kept their toes tucked against the ledge.

"Want to switch colours?" Dani asked, offering me the blue. "I'm going to pop these out of the tin."

"Brook, give me your finger." I looked to the small raven-haired soul that was eyeballing the cupcakes.

She put her whole hand out, all fingers pointed my direction.

I piped a small swirl of the purple icing onto her first two fingers. "Go ahead."

"Fable? Do you want some?" I asked as I placed the purple icing bag, which was nearly empty, on the far end of the counter near where Danielle had left the bowl of blue icing.

"BLUE!" she exclaimed, making her request and holding out two fingers.

I smiled as I picked up the fresh bag and made a little swirl for her.

"Sure, ice cream, icing, they're going to be wild tonight." Danielle rolled her eyes.

"I'm not sorry." I shrugged, enjoying seeing the girls licking the sweetness off, their tongues turning their respective colours.

"Do you want me to take your dog?" I heard behind me as Phillip appeared in cleaner clothes. All signs of construction dust had been erased.

I looked toward the doorway to my suite. "No, but thank you. I think I should go home to them shortly."

Danielle gave me a look. "You can go whenever. Thank you for your help."

I smiled, having enjoyed the unexpected surprise. "Thank you, I love spending time with the girls."

"Come on! Let's go!" Phillip picked up each of his children and returned them to the ground as they giggled.

"Enjoy!" I called as they walked out the door.

Danielle and I worked in silence for a while, both knowing that anything said could be overheard.

I finished the last dozen of the remaining chocolate cupcakes in blue icing.

As I put down the bag, Dani looked at me. "Don't accept less than you deserve, Hallie."

At her words, I had to fight back tears as I leaned against the counter.

"How do I know what the threshold is?" I asked quietly with a wavering voice.

"You deserve someone who wants to be a part of your world," she said, pointedly looking out the front window to where Phillip and the girls had passed a few minutes earlier on their walk to get 'insurance'.

She was right. It felt like a personal slight that my little family up here didn't matter to him at all, though he knew how much I adored them.

What part of me did he still adore? If I thought about it, I didn't know anymore.

Three Little Things

S TANDING OUTSIDE THE ENTRANCE to our suite, I took a deep breath to centre myself.

I had an unsettling feeling about opening the door and wanted to delay the action just a few more moments.

I took another breath before moving my hand to the handle and entering my home.

"Hey!" I called down the stairs.

Riggley appeared with tail wagging, but I otherwise received silence.

Removing my shoes, I crept down the stairs to meet Rigs and followed him to the front of the suite.

Jordan sat on the couch with his head in his hands. Riggley passed me to scale the couch and began licking his dad's covered face.

My heart dropped. Seeing him in distress always upset me.

I slowly moved to sit between him and Rigs on the couch.

Sitting quietly with him for a moment, I pet Riggley to calm him and waited for Jordan to lift his face from his hands so I could talk to him. Jordan stayed where he was, unmoving.

"Hey Love." I said, putting a hand on his shoulder after a few moments. "What's the matter?"

Jordan kept his face in his hands, but his breathing changed. It became heavier, hitched. I rested a hand on his back, waiting for an answer.

After several seconds without one, I opted for a kiss on his shoulder and got up to start the kettle. Jordan liked tea and I hoped a cup would help. I noted that Jordan had picked up groceries as some of the nonperishables were still in bags on the counter.

I pulled two mugs from the cupboard before turning back to sit beside Jordan as the water heated up. Rigs stayed with his dad, snuggling closer and resting his chin on Jordan's thigh.

Finally, he put his hands down on his lap and I could see his face. His cheeks were streaked with tears and his eyes were red. He didn't look sad, he looked serious. I moved to grab him a tissue and sat beside him again. He took the tissue and dried his eyes.

Jordan inhaled a deep breath and then looked at me. "You cleaned the room."

"I did," I replied, trying to sound positive. "I spent all afternoon on it, and I made us a yoga den!"

Jordan didn't exactly respond; rather, he continued to look at me as though he was searching for an answer in my eyes. He sighed, then put his face back into his hands. My heart rate quickened his reaction.

"What happened today?" I probed, becoming more worried.

"Nothing," he mumbled.

"Then why are you upset?"

"I'm fine."

"You're fine..."

"Yes. Leave it alone, Hallie."

The kettle was boiling. I got up and picked a chamomile tea for both of us. I let it steep for a few minutes, choosing to stay at the kitchen counter. When the tea smelled fragrant with the calming floral scent, and the water was coloured, I took the tea bags out and returned to the couch.

Jordan took one look at the cup that was offered to him and said, "I don't want that. Also, what the hell did you do with our coffee table?"

I paused, still holding both cups. "I borrowed the coffee table. It's in the spare room."

Jordan looked at me again, with the same searching expression. This time he mocked me as he spoke, "you just do what you like with our things, don't you?"

I wasn't entirely surprised by the sudden turn of his attitude. I took a moment before speaking, "I don't know what you mean ..."

"Why did you decide to take over the spare room?" he asked.

I paused, wanting to be careful with my words.

Moving to sit at the table, I put our mugs down before pulling out a stool and reluctantly taking a seat. "We weren't using it... I just cleaned everything up so that I could use it as a space to practice yoga at home."

"Why did you need to steal the coffee table?" he asked, waving at the empty space in front of the couch.

"Because I wanted an altar... I can put it back."

"An altar?" he scoffed. "Are you performing witchcraft or something?"

I hadn't thought of an altar like that. To me, it was just a place to put my crystals and trinkets to make the room feel like a sacred space, but I guess it was a little ritualistic. I wasn't sure how to respond so I stayed silent.

There were a few moments of quiet tension before Jordan spoke again. "I thought we were going to create that space together..."

My heart pinged with the feeling of guilt.

"I didn't mean to take anything over," I said quietly. "I had the inspiration to clean things up today and I thought it would be nice to have a home studio for a while."

"I don't want a room in our house that's only yours and I'm not allowed to use it," he said curtly.

"Of course you can use it, Jordan. It's not *my* room. I just finally did something with it," I told him. I picked up my tea which was now cool enough to drink and took a sip.

"So you'll be okay with me moving some equipment in there now that it's clean?"

I paused. Jordan made it seem like he wanted to create the space 'together', but his suggestions also made my intentions for it unusable. He had talked about treadmills and machines which would take up all the space. It was not a big room. His comment felt more like a challenge than a question.

"I'd like to use the space as a yoga studio for a while," I replied steadily. "You can add some dumbbells and stuff in there, but if you put in any large equipment then I won't be able to use it."

"So it's still all about you, huh?" he said savagely.

"Excuse me?" I replied, shocked.

"You heard me." Jordan looked at me with hard eyes. I knew this wasn't about me, or the room but I couldn't help getting fired up.

"You could have cleaned the room, too!" I shot back defensively. "It's been unused for months. I tidied it so it could finally be enjoyed. It made me happy today. It's not my fault you're in a sour mood right now and won't choose to enjoy it with me."

"I'm in a sour mood?" he said. "You're clueless."

I did not appreciate the way he was talking to me. My empathy toward him was being tested and he was projecting whatever frustration he had walked in with onto me. It wasn't fair.

"I asked what was going on. I offered you tea. I'm here if you want to talk," I said firmly, avoiding the jab.

"I don't want to talk. I want you to bring the damn coffee table back." Jordan got up from the couch and moved toward me. He grabbed his cup and said, "Thanks for the tea."

His gratitude dripped with sarcasm.

He took a sip and walked past me to the bedroom. At this point, I lost all sympathy for him. Whatever had ruined his day was his own problem. "What's your deal, Jordan?"

"Pardon me?"

"You come in all angry and sad and you take it out on me without telling me what's the matter. This isn't about the room. It's about your day. What happened today?" I asked again, getting up from my own seat as Riggley lifted his head, watching the exchange.

"Nothing. Happened. Today," Jordan said in a hard tone. He continued to walk to the bedroom with his back to me.

I stood in the kitchen staring down the hallway as he moved through the doorway into the room we shared, in disbelief at the way he was talking to me. The contempt in his voice was cutting.

I didn't want to follow him, and he clearly didn't want to be followed. It felt awkward standing at the table by myself, sipping my tea. Instead, I went to sit on the couch beside Riggley. I reached for the remote but stopped before turning the TV on. The sound would probably bother him.

This was a familiar experience. Jordan and I often got into arguments to the point where the tension between us was unbearable. Trapped in my own home, I felt caught in a cage of resentment and hurt feelings. Jordan came out of the bedroom and into the kitchen, saying nothing. I could feel his frustration like a heavy pressure in the air. I didn't dare make another comment.

He pointedly put away the remaining groceries in silence before looking at my breakfast dishes which were still in the sink, then at the clean dishwasher. He stubbornly refused to turn his attention to me despite seeing the small mess I had made earlier in the day. Instead, he opened the dishwasher and began to empty the racks.

Guilt hit me. I had been home all day working on the spare bedroom and had left our chores forgotten. It was irrational because I had indeed run the dishwasher that morning, but a heaviness settled in my chest anyway. I sipped the tea I now cradled in my hands.

A flush of heat rushed to my face. I was about to cry, and it wasn't because of the dishes. The anxiety in my chest was about to reach its threshold at the space that was forming between us. Jordan's attention remained focused on the dishes. It was as though my presence in the room was nonexistent.

I wanted to run. I wanted to hide somewhere where I could cry this out without having Jordan bear witness but in such a small suite, there was nowhere I could go where he wouldn't be able to walk in on my tears.

My tea was nearly done. I finished the last sips and held the empty cup for a moment. The tension became unbearable as I watched my boyfriend clean the kitchen and intentionally ignore me.

Jordan had finished both the top and bottom racks and now pulled out the utensil caddy. I got up from the couch to put my teacup in the newly emptied dishwasher. As he put the utensils away, I finished washing out the cup from the yogurt and placed it under the sink in the white veneer drawer that pulled out and revealed our recycling. The spoon I had used to eat my yogurt and granola was still in the sink as well. I waited awkwardly for Jordan to finish with the utensils, and when he did, I offered the spoon. He still didn't look at me. Instead, he offered the caddy for me to take. I put the spoon in the caddy then took it so I could return it to its place in the dishwasher. As I put the extended racks back into the machine and closed it, I could see Jordan walk back to the bedroom out of my peripheral vision.

As soon as he was out of sight, the tears that had been threatening started filling my eyes. I couldn't take this anymore. I needed to get out of this house.

I wiped my face and walked to the spare room to grab my favourite crystal for comfort. The space felt less special than it had an hour ago. As I collected my crystal from the altar, Jordan once again moved to the kitchen. I took the opportunity to grab my hoodie and my car keys from our bedroom and my parka from the hall closet.

I knew he would hear the jingle of my car keys and the sound of me putting on my boots at the door. Riggley did. He wagged his tail at the base of the stairs, looking at me with concerned eyes. I wanted to kiss his sweet face, but I stuck to our routine.

I didn't want to just leave Jordan which would feel rude and petty, so I called out, "I'll be back in a little bit."

I paused, before adding, "I love you…"

Silence.

Sigh.

My boots were on and my keys were in hand, so I opened the door and walked out into the crisp, black night. The dampness around my eyes stung in the cold air.

I got in my car and drove myself to a nearby coffee shop. Tears left wet trails on my face the whole way there, but once I was sitting in the little booth with a steaming mug of vanilla steamed milk in my hands, I felt much better. The anxiety in my chest had subsided and my thoughts weren't muddled with emotion.

During these bouts of silent treatment, it became a dance of avoidance. Each of us would move in ways that circumvented direct contact with the other. I quietly refrained from engaging with him out of fear of exacerbating the argument or triggering another wave of negative interaction.

This round had little to do with me. It couldn't. The spare room must be a scapegoat for something tied to this early return from work.

This dance became our typical routine once the silent treatment started. I would usually leave the house for a couple of hours to let Jordan process whatever he needed to and to give myself a chance to clear my head as well. Being in the same space as each other with the heavy weight of emotional discord felt intolerable for me, and Jordan never ended up the one to break the silence. We would talk when I was home again and ready to make reparations. It was seemingly always up to me to bridge the silence into communication, but I wasn't always sure I did well with the responsibility.

Sometimes I would take myself out to dinner during these escapes, but I always worried that Jordan would make dinner for two while I was gone. Maybe he wouldn't make dinner at all. I never knew what to expect when I got back home and didn't want to eat without him if I could help it.

I rubbed my eyes. It had been about an hour, and I was finished my steamed milk. It was time to go back. The worse the argument, the longer I usually stayed away from the house. This one had escalated quickly and brought up some serious anxiety, but after my warm drink, I was calm enough to return.

On the short drive home, I considered my tactic for getting us to resume dialogue. I figured a gentle approach would be the best as I knew he had a hard day. I repeated to myself that this wasn't about me today.

When I walked in the door, I could feel that the atmosphere had calmed. Riggley didn't even bark as I entered the house. I took a deep breath and took off my shoes before putting my coat away and walking toward the kitchen. Jordan wasn't there. I checked the bedroom. It was empty.

Thinking Jordan took Rigs for a walk, I started making dinner for two.

It was unusual for me to cook for the two of us, as Jordan enjoyed more elaborate fare than I enjoyed putting the effort into. I did enjoy cooking, but Jordan often seemed to make suggestions for how I could improve my technique or add more flavour.

Despite this historical pattern, I moved to the fridge and investigated what Jordan had brought home. Rummaging around the new inventory, I picked out some chicken and veggies.

When I finished making our dinner and the smell of cooked carrots and savoury spices filled the kitchen, the door opened from the spare room.

I hadn't even thought to check for Jordan in there! I had been home for a solid half hour. What had he been doing?

Riggley emerged, trotting over to me with his tail swishing. Behind him, Jordan came into the kitchen and made eye contact with me. I relaxed. A good sign.

"I made dinner," I said. "There's enough for both of us."

Jordan looked at the baking sheet I had just pulled out of the oven. "You didn't need to."

The comment triggered the part of me that could do no right with him, however, he was talking. Also a good sign.

"I didn't know if you were home, and I was hungry."

We pulled plates out of the cupboards and each took a share of the meal. We sat down together at the high table and ate.

I noticed Jordan shredding the chicken over the first few bites. As expected, after a few more, Jordan got up and procured balsamic vinegar and oil from the cupboard above the stove. He moved to the fridge and got some Dijon mustard and mayonnaise. I watched as he grabbed a small ramekin from the drawers beside the table and brown sugar from the cupboards above.

As I continued to eat the meal I thought was delicious and well-cooked, he mixed an elaborate dressing, finishing it off with lemon zest.

He returned to the table and poured the dressing over the shredded chicken.

I ate my feelings on the matter, focusing on the meal rather than the message he was silently sending. Our dinner was consumed in silence, but I reminded myself, at least we were in the same room.

It was not entirely silent in the house, though.

Cries could be heard coming from the stairs.

Brook.

It must be dinnertime for them as well. Tantrums were a common commotion at this time of day.

Jordan kept his eyes on his plate, refraining from making a comment and acting like he heard nothing. I wondered if he had caught the exchange between Phillip and I as he came home but decided that it was not my concern if he did.

When both our plates were empty, I got up and put them away in the dishwasher. When I was done, I squared my shoulders and chose to let my irritation subside with the greater goal of establishing peace.

"I realize you came home to a bit of a surprise today," I said, turning to face him and beginning to address the issue of the spare room. "I know I didn't talk to you before I did it, but I felt motivated today. I hope it's okay..."

Jordan said nothing for a moment, he just looked at his hands on the table. "I just wish you would have involved me. You moved all my things, and when I got home, I felt like you essentially claimed the room for yourself."

His words made me feel like I had been selfish with my actions. A hint of shame that I had done what I wanted to do with the room instead of allowing Jordan to do the same touched my heart. "I still want you to be able to use it. Did you? I noticed you were in there."

Jordan nodded, still looking at his hands. His voice was tight. "I meditated for a little bit to calm down."

His response to my arrival back at the house seemed more receptive than usual. I was glad he had chosen to use the space instead of avoiding it.

"I still want the coffee table back in the living room," he said. "But I liked that you had our old photos on it."

I smiled, glad he had noticed. "See? It's for both of us."

Jordan finally looked up at me. He held eye contact for a brief moment before his breath hitched and he looked away. Jordan started to sob.

This time, I didn't hesitate. I put a hand on his back and kissed his shoulder.

"What's the matter, love? What happened today?"

I gave Jordan a few minutes to express his emotions, knowing that he was finally in a space where I could talk to him. I got up to grab another tissue. It was the last one in the box. When I returned to the table, I took Jordan's hand. "Come to the couch. We can talk for a little bit."

Jordan allowed me to lead him over to where it was more comfortable and as we sat down, I curled up into his chest, not allowing him to put his head in his hands like he usually would as a response to stress.

I could feel him taking deep breaths to collect himself.

Riggley appeared beside the couch. He had been sleeping in his crate while we ate dinner but was now an empathetic puddle at our feet.

"I don't know what's wrong, or why I feel like this, but I keep thinking that I'm letting everyone down and I can't make it stop," he said, his voice shaky.

"That's quite the negative thing to be saying to yourself." I replied, trying to remain neutral. "What's bringing this on?"

"I don't know, that's the thing. But I feel it at work, I feel it with you, I feel it all the time. It's crushing me." Jordan shifted and I responded by sitting up, wanting to look at his face as I asked my next question.

"Why do you feel like you're letting me down?' I asked.

Jordan went to put his head in his hands again. I quickly put my hands in his and drew them into my lap. "Look at me, please."

He sighed and lifted his gaze to meet mine. He looked exhausted. I knew that we both felt the consequences of our arguments and this was a tough topic to talk about. I tried to make sure my expression was calm and inviting.

"I just feel like we're constantly at war and that's not how a relationship should be. We should be happy. We should be a team. We should be doing things together."

I could tell he was expressing his frustrations toward the spare room again and I wanted desperately to avoid this heart-to-heart turning into a heated argument.

Jordan continued in my silence. "I love you, Hallie. I would feel lost without you. I feel like if I fail you, then I've failed the relationship, and I've failed myself."

"You can't think of it like that," I advised. "I love you too, Jordan, but that's not a healthy way of looking at it."

"I know," he said. "It's just how I feel."

I let go of his hands and leaned forward to put my head on his shoulder. Jordan and I had both been experiencing signs of depression for months. We were both suffering through our arguments, but this internal conflict concerned me even though I understood it well. I didn't know what caused it for him but still wanted to support him through the struggle.

"I think you need to have a little more faith in yourself, love," I said gently. "I see the strong, steady partner I chose to be with behind whatever it is that you're going through. I need you to see it, too."

"How do I do that?" he asked, his tone sounded defeated.

I thought for a moment. "Can you tell me three things that you like about yourself? Three qualities that you appreciate or are proud of?"

Jordan paused, saying nothing. I thought this exercise would help to lift his mood and generate confidence.

To my surprise, Jordan's breath caught in his chest again. He didn't answer me. Instead, he started breathing heavier. Jordan went from small, hitched breaths to deep inhales. His face contorted into a look of agony. A few sobs spiraled into a full, devastating bawl. He shook me off and put his palms to his eyes again.

Instead of helping it seemed like my words had done harm. I was alarmed.

"Jordan! Jordan, you're okay!" I pleaded with him, wrapping my arms around his frame. "It's okay."

"No it's not," he said through tears. "I don't have anything that I like about myself. Nothing."

I was shocked by how dark of a place he must be in. "Oh, Jordan... I could list so many about you."

"I can't Hallie. I just can't." He shook me off.

I sat in silence beside him, processing. I figured this was just a bad time to ask. He was emotional and in a negative headspace. Surely he would be able to list these things when he was calm and collected.

"Okay, Jordan. You don't have to," I said, refraining from reaching out to him again.

We sat for another few moments, letting him steady his breathing and wipe his tears away with the now crumpled, worn tissue.

Once Jordan was calm, we cleaned the kitchen together and the three of us went to bed.

I wanted so badly to tell Jordan what was going on within my heart but the weight of it was significant. Jordan's emotional well-being seemed to be in a precarious place, and I didn't want to add the stress of a possible breakup. My emotions hadn't fully processed yet either, so now was not the right time.

There was no rush. It would be impulsive to act on the message without allowing myself the time to move through the emotions I felt because of it first.

You, alone.

There were moments where I doubted that I had received the message correctly. I would remember the feeling of The Universe shutting Jordan out of my thoughts though, and knew I understood perfectly well.

Maybe this was a 'not right now'. I was still so in love with Jordan I hoped this could mean that our paths were just not meant to be together for this period in time. Maybe the two of us both needed room to grow and learn before one day we would come together again.

That was a possibility... right?

I wanted to spin this in some way so that I got both the things I wanted. I wanted to keep Jordan, but I also strongly desired to explore this promise The Universe had alluded to.

I didn't want to lose him.

My hopes were high that even if I went through with the message, perhaps I could do so delicately enough to preserve the connection we shared.

I wondered if I had the resolve, the strength, the compassion, and the empathy needed to save this. What would it take of me to proceed with caution and care?

What more could dare to come between us?

Life Warms My Feet
Curled Tight With Signs of Sleep
A Dream Has Stirred My Second Shadow
His Legs On My Legs
We Must Be Running

Audacious Dawn

DAYS TURNED TO WEEKS as I ignored the message of my Journey. One of my girlfriends, Maxille, reached out one Sunday and asked if I wanted to go for a hike. The cold weather had finally began transitioning to spring and we had been enjoying some rather beautiful days.

Jordan was home on the last of his days off but had plans already with friends, so I left Riggley behind with him as I made hiking my own plan for the day.

Banff National Park was in my metaphorical backyard. The mountain town was only a little over an hour outside of my city. It was my favourite place in the world.

Max and I had been friends for several years, and we were frequently trying to get ourselves out to the mountains. We met before a music festival I was attending with Jordan and a few of his friends. Jordan's friends had hosted a pre-game party, where Max found me in the bathroom putting on makeup.

She appeared suddenly, introduced herself, and offered to put my eyelashes on for me. We bonded quickly while talking about yoga, breathwork, the mountains, and doe-eyed vs. cat-eye lash arrangements. We have been friends ever since.

"Hello, my dearest and sincerest pal!" Max said as I opened the car door. She was always saying the silliest phrases.

"Hello, Lovely," I responded, laughing at what I saw on my seat.

On it was a metal bowl (it was an insert from a rice maker) full of whole fruits and vegetables I had to lift onto my lap in order to sit down.

"Snacks for the roaaaad!" Max sang. It was so typical of her. I called her my 'Wicker Basket Girl' because she gave off hippie grandmotherly gardener vibes. Her colour palette was earthy browns and dusty yellows. She and I shared so many features we could be sisters, except Maxille had a short black bob which sharpened her look. She had brought the fruit and veggie basket on every hike I had been on with her.

"I'll save the potassium rockets for the hike!" I joked, picking up a banana. I loved hanging out with Max because I could be entirely myself around her. Her comical mannerisms were infectious and provided a safe space for me to behave the same.

We started talking about life as soon as she pulled away from my house.

"I'm moving into a new place! I'll be a lot closer to you now," Max began. She was currently living on the outskirts of the city.

"That's exciting! When do you move?"

"Start of June!" she replied.

"Are you moving in with roommates, or maybe a boyfriend?" I asked, prying for juicy details.

"Just roommates." Max rolled her eyes. "How are you and Jordan doing?"

"Ugh, girl, don't even." I put my hands over my eyes. Embarrassment settled on the periphery of my emotions even though I knew she would hold my problems with delicate care. "Jordan and I are fine for right now but I'm starting to embrace my spiritual journey and it feels like Jordan is getting left behind."

"Oh?" Max said, reaching for an apple from the basket in my lap.

"I think The Universe is trying to wake me up and shake me into doing more with my life but I'm not sure what just yet."

"I went through something similar," Max sympathized. "I mean, about The Universe's wake-up calls."

Max told her story as I listened intently.

"I was in a corporate job that I thought was supposed to be my future," she began. "I had gone to school for it and thought I was settling into a long career. One morning I woke up from a dream. I was at work, and everything was business as usual. I was writing a note on my desk, and when I read what I was writing the note said: *change is coming*. Suddenly the walls began to melt, and the room began to spin and the whole scene disappeared."

The crunch of Maxille's apple broke her story.

"There is nothing I could have done after that to hold my job. I began making small mistakes that turned into gigantic issues. I started getting vertigo and needed to take some time off. When I came back, the feeling of satisfaction I had with my job was gone. I hated it. I wanted out. I wanted *more*."

Max took her eyes off the road to glance at me quickly. "You will find your path. It won't be easy, but it will be worth it. It won't look anything like you expect it to, but it will take you exactly where you need to be."

I looked up at Max, surprised. She had never talked about this part of her history before. Max was a few years older than me, but I was surprised she had fit all of that into the years before I had known her. She'd been a yoga teacher for as long as we had been friends.

"You can do this, girl."

"Thank you, Lovely. I'm doing my best to let it unfold. I still haven't told Jordan." I moved the basket of fruit from my lap to the floor beside my feet. "I want to, but I don't think he's ready to hear it and I don't think I'm ready to share yet."

"Everything will happen exactly as it's meant to. It's a universal law. Don't worry your pretty little head about the details. Just let it flow."

Maxille closed the conversation by reaching back behind me to dispose of her apple core in a little bag attached to my seat belt holster.

I nodded. 'Letting it flow' was something that I was working on. I liked to feel like I had a sense of control over my environment. The idea that I needed to relax into the bigger picture of my Journey instead of the details was a concept that gave me anxiety. I wanted to have the details sorted neatly and beautifully packaged.

We arrived at the Grassi Lakes trailhead minutes before noon, and I was stunned. There was nearly a kilometre of vehicles parked along the side of the road. We stalked some hikers who were on their way back to their car and waited for them to leave so that we could take their parking spot.

When we got on the trail it was packed with every tourist and their dog. I turned to Max. "This is insane!"

"I know!" she replied, dodging someone who was coming down the mountain. "This is one of the first nice weekends of the year, though, so I guess everyone is capitalizing on it."

"It's the long weekend," a woman behind us said, explaining everything. She was close enough to hear our conversation.

There was still the occasional patch of ice on the ground which was making things slippery. The trail was so busy that the two of us had to go single file, and slowly. I could tell Max was getting frustrated and so was I.

"Do you want to keep going?" I asked. We had been on the trail for less than half the journey.

"I wanted to show you the lakes," Max replied, looking ahead.

"I know, I want to see them, too…" I nearly tripped on the rocks under my feet. I couldn't see them coming.

Suddenly, Max slipped and fell hard.

"Are you okay?" I rushed to her side. She brushed herself off and stood up quickly to get off the trail.

Max and I pulled off to the side of the trail to let the other hikers pass us. We talked for a few minutes about whether we wanted to keep going and decided that it wasn't a good day to be on the trail.

I didn't like 'giving up' on a hike, especially one this easy, but there were so many people it wasn't enjoyable for either of us. I had heard that these lakes were gorgeous, but I didn't see myself being able to appreciate them when they were crowded with tourists and other hikers.

We headed back down the mountain, shuffling through the oncoming hikers still heading toward the lake. When we got back to the car I sighed in relief. I wondered if I had some underlying claustrophobia because being shuffled up that hill had been anxiety inducing.

"Are you okay?" I asked Max again, thinking about her fall.

"Yes! I don't think I injured anything!" she said as she started the car.

We drove to the little mountain town so that we could at least make use of the day. There were shops along the main avenue and a coffee shop we liked to go to after our hikes. We ended up going for a long walk by the river flowing through the town, ending up at a set of waterfalls.

"La vie est belle," Max said as we looked at the water rushing over the rocks.

She was right, life was beautiful.

Max dropped me off in the late afternoon, leaving me with a whole red pepper.

Jordan was home. His bags were already packed by the base of the stairs, blocking Riggley's usual spot. He was returning for a shift at work later tonight.

Since our last argument, we had been able to find some peace.

I finally showed him the affection he was looking for and now understood the gravity of his feelings of failure. I had done my best in the days since to be kind and receptive, and I could tell he was making an effort to tone down the sarcastic remarks.

"How was the hike?" Jordan was in the kitchen prepping dinner.

"Didn't make it," I sighed. "May Long. Terrible timing."

"Oh?" he inquired.

"So busy. Still icy. Terrible timing!" I reinforced as I took out my water bottle and put my backpack in the hall closet with Riggly wiggling beside me.

Moving to the kitchen to empty the water bottle, I assessed what may be on the menu for tonight.

Jordan was in the middle of wrapping bacon around asparagus spears. There was a pot on the stove with its lid tipped at an angle.

"How was your day?" I asked.

"Good, not looking forward to leaving." The expression on his face confirmed his hesitation.

"Has work been going okay?" I asked, thinking of his previous return.

"Yeah, things are fine. Just gotta keep pushing through the travel. I want to be home more." His words seemed to be evading depth in his answer.

Jordan hadn't opened up about his unexpectedly early return home, but it hadn't happened again since.

I had all sorts of suspicions as to why he was struggling internally, but none of them were confirmed. It seemed as though both of us were hiding our inner worlds from the other.

As Jordan pulled out marinated chicken from the fridge, I noted that there were also eggs and flour prepared for breading the chicken.

From the far kitchen counter, I pulled out the treats for Riggley, hoping to work on 'Crawl' again.

The moment Rigs heard the treats rustle, he was at my side.

I signaled for 'Sit'. He sat.

I signaled for 'Lay Down'. He lay down.

I signaled for 'Stay' and started walking back toward the bedrooms. He stayed.

"Okay!" I released him. He raced down the hallway to receive his reward.

I lowered my hand to give him one of the treats and rub his ears as he ate it.

I started out by putting him in a 'Sit' and a 'Stay', and then lined the treats on the ground again, trying to leave a little more space between the treats to encourage the crawling motion.

"Lay down," I told him, standing behind him. He immediately went to get the first treat thinking he was released.

I grabbed his collar and pulled him back. "Lay down" I reinforced with a firm tone.

Riggley lay down.

"Crawl," I told him as I held his hips down.

Riggley began to crawl.

"Yes!" I said as he reached each treat. "Crawl!" I encouraged as he moved toward the next one.

He reached the last treat. I clapped twice, made my "Yesss!" more cheerful, and fetched a small tidbit of turkey from the deli drawer.

Keeping in mind his previous training session, I wanted to keep this positive.

"All done!" I clapped my hands open to let Riggley know I wasn't going to ask him to do any more and gifted him with the cold morsel of poultry.

Riggley got up and licked my fingers, searching for any remaining flavour.

Jordan had been watching us in the hallway as he was cooking the chicken.

"You're doing really well with him," he commented as I passively led Rigs back into the dining area.

I sat on one of the high chairs from the table that I hated. "Thank you. I think he's been doing a lot better for us coming home. All I've been doing is adding structure and consistency."

"I've noticed. He doesn't howl or get in the way at the top of the stairs." Jordan's remark made me smile.

At least he noticed what I was doing for our family and was not in a space where he was taking my turn of attention personally.

"What's for dinner?" I asked, seeing new pots on the stove.

"Chicken parm with polenta and asparagus." Jordan took a look in the oven window. "The chicken just needs a few more minutes and a layer of cheese and then we're done."

I did appreciate the meals he made. I just wish I could contribute without it seeming to be insufficient.

As I went to reach for my phone that I had left on the counter, it started to vibrate.

DONATEBLOOD showed up on the call screen.

The number had been calling me for weeks and I hadn't been ready to answer the call. Donating blood was something I'd done throughout my adult life, and often Jordan and I tried to do it together. With us being at odds for so long, life seemed too chaotic for me to make an appointment, but I had been feeling more in tune with my regular routines.

"Do you want to come with me to donate blood?" I asked.

Jordan shook his head as he spread a layer of cheese on the chicken. "I'm still on T."

I answered the call, making an appointment for tomorrow because they were in urgent demand for donors as per the agent on the phone.

Jordan set the timer on the stove for five minutes.

"What are you going to get up to while I'm away?" he asked.

I hadn't thought about it.

"I think I'll stay at home with Rigs for the most part. Go for some walks. Donate blood now, apparently."

He nodded, pensively, still standing at the oven.

"Why, what's up?" I asked.

Jordan took exactly seven seconds too long to answer.

I counted them as the stove timer went from 1:18 to 1:11.

He looked down at the oven window. "Just thought I'd ask."

Alarm bells raised. He was excellent at saying nothing and too much at the same time.

Caught between wanting to know what was causing such distress, wanting to show I cared to ask, and wanting desperately to avoid an argument, I took fifteen seconds of my own to come to a decision.

In the moments I took, Jordan pulled the pan of chicken from the oven.

I inhaled the warm scent of breading and tomato sauce.

If I was still keeping my secrets, then I decided that he could keep his also. I didn't need to pry just at this moment.

Jordan plated dinner and I set down cutlery at the table.

I hoisted myself into the seat, waiting in silence, watching my partner across the kitchen.

What was going through his mind? Was his secret the cause of his distress, and I was just an outlet for the frustration? Could I afford to give him some grace as we moved through this unknown challenge together?

You, *alone*.

The message of my Journey rung in my mind like an unwanted visitor in that moment. I wanted this to work!

Jordan turned to bring the plates to the table just then.

He must have caught the expression of frustrated concentration on my face as his head tilted slightly to the right as he saw me.

We both chose to say nothing. To maintain the silence on behalf of the other's secrets. To not open doors to paths we didn't want to go down.

The dinner, though, was delicious.

Something about the polenta paired so well with the chicken and tomato and cheese. It was creamy, it was textured, it was rich.

I leaned over to Jordan and offered him a kiss on the shoulder.

"I've never had chicken parm," I confided, with my lips against his shoulder. "But this is the best one I've ever had."

"Thanks, Hallie." He turned his head to kiss mine. "I appreciate that."

Jordan left after dinner as I cleaned up the kitchen. If he made me such a lovely dinner for us to share, the least I could do was tidy up after it.

Upon finishing, I spent a little bit of time in the spare room with Riggley. The coffee table had been returned to the living room as requested last week.

As I sat in meditation, a restlessness settled over me, my mind ruminating over what Jordan might be hiding from me. What could be going so wrong in his world that he felt everything hinged on my love for him?

Eventually, I gave up trying to calm the thoughts that seemed to stubbornly want to remain in an uncertain cycle.

I went to bed.

I could not sleep.

These nights occurred every few weeks or so. I would go to bed at a decent hour, but my mind refused to slip away into unconsciousness.

It was well past midnight when suddenly I was struck by an idea.

I was still awake, so why didn't I make use of it? The trail Max and I had hiked today came to mind. I bet if I went at dawn there would be hardly a soul ambitious enough to start hiking so early. A sunrise hike had been on my bucket list for years, but I had yet to have the inspiration to go.

I got out of bed and put on some clothes.

Riggley was at my side, curious of what I was up to.

"Wanna go for a hike?" I asked him.

Immediate tail swishes responded.

I grabbed my adventure pack and emptied it from my last excursion. This time I packed it with a cedar bundle, my quartz crystal, a flashlight, my camera, and a tripod.

I stood at the bottom of the stairs, waiting for my shadow to calm himself and sit.

When he did, I ascended the stairs, opened the door, and released my pup. He raced up the stairs and spun circles around me as I locked the deadbolt.

It was still dark but I knew dawn was not far away. I didn't leash Riggley for the short walk to the car. He led the way.

I opened the back of my little hatchback to let Rigs in. He made the jump effortlessly and turned back for kisses now that he was on my level. I gave him some scritches under the chin before closing the hatch and making my way to the driver's side. Sliding into my seat, I started the car and turned on some quiet music. I backed out of my parking pad and after a few turns was headed toward the mountains.

As I drove, all I could think about was the possibility that we would get eaten by a cougar. I knew that they were most active at twilight and dawn, and I was a single female hiker about to be alone in the woods. Riggley would protect me, but I also didn't want him to become a target.

The roads were clear of other drivers and my travels were peaceful. When I arrived at the parking lot leading up to the trailhead, it was empty. The quiet was a stark contrast to the lineup of vehicles and hikers weaving between them that I had experienced earlier.

The sky was turning from a deep navy to a royal blue. I sat in my car with Rigs gently whining to be let out, deciding that I didn't want to hike by the light of my flashlight. I searched up cougar attacks on my phone as I waited for the sky to brighten. As I read articles about how to defend yourself in the event of different predator encounters, I realized that I should have brought a weapon of some sort or at least a can of bear spray.

I couldn't believe I was about to do this.

Despite not sleeping all night, I was wide awake. When the sky was finally a light blue and I could see the features of the path in front of me clearly, I got out of my car. No one had arrived at the parking lot yet, and I felt pleased that I would be the first one on the trail that morning.

I let Rigs out of the hatch of my car, clipping the retractable leash to his collar and looking toward the path.

I was nervous to be on the trail alone but ventured to the edge of the lot, casting a brief glance at the sign marking the trailhead and into the trees.

As I walked, I came across a stick on the ground that looked pointy enough to be used in self-defence. I picked it up.

My attention remained aware of my surroundings, looking through the trees for any sign of predators.

It was odd, to fear coming across something unwanted alone in the woods. I kept watch on the trees to my left and right, trying to see deeper than what was in front of me. There was a barrier, though, where the depth of the trees abruptly made them seem like a wall I could not view past.

It felt like my life. I could see only so far into the woods, limited by where I was on the trail and how dense the trees became. There was only so far of a radius where I could know what was in front of me. Even though I had been on this part of the trail yesterday, it was familiar but distinctly different. A new experience of it.

Riggley walked well on the path, leading the way, sniffing everything but respecting the tension on the leash as I followed. The trail felt roomy as I continued upward. I had the entire space between the trees and shrubs on either side of me all to myself.

I remained concerned about the trees, and what may lurk unseen. It was this unknown, this possibility of danger that made me uneasy and watchful over my radius. I looked behind me many times to ensure nothing stalked me where past steps left my scent on the trail.

It was a crisp morning, though I was surprised by how warm it was. I was comfortable wearing a light jacket and even unzipped after I started working up a delicate sweat. I could hear birds singing and squirrels calling to each other through the trees.

We had hiked for about a half hour when the path became a delta of channels through the trees. I could see the glistening blue water just a few meters in front of me.

Choosing my way, I stepped out of the foliage to the shores of a small but stunning lake. I was in a pass between two mountains which framed my view of the cyan waters in front of me.

Maxille and I must have been close before we turned back. It had felt like we were on the trail for much longer.

The sky was bright and the clouds were beginning to colour, but the sun had not yet risen above the mountain range across the valley.

Riggley and I walked around the edge of the lake. It was crystal clear. I could see trees resting at the bottom and rocks covered in a layer of green algae. Wooden walkways edged the lake, and we took this path slowly as I embraced my surroundings. It was so peaceful, so serene.

I stood at the edge of the water, balancing on the shore and a stone as I dipped my fingers into the chill. The water was frigid, reminding me of the barrier within my Journey, aware that I was able to penetrate this surface.

I removed my hands and flicked them to dispel the water before wiping them on my joggers to dry.

There was a second lake, just above the first. Beautifully constructed bridges made of whole, bark-covered logs separated the two glimmering bodies of water.

Rigs and I continued to explore and discovered a rocky trail behind the upper lake, leading into the pass between the mountains. We followed the winding trail as the mountains drew closer on either side. Eventually, the path hit an outcropping of rocks that could be climbed.

I tied Rigs to a stumpy tree near the base of the rocks. He whined as I found footholds and crevices and began to ascend a large boulder. I wasn't much of a rock climber, but this appeared simple and there were natural tiers in the rock which made my attempt to scale it easier.

When I arrived at the top, I was in awe. My view looked over the lakes below and the river valley beyond that. The undersides of the clouds were streaked with deep oranges and pastel pinks. The sun was just appearing as a sliver above the mountains in front of me.

This was one of those moments worth living for.

I sat down on the rock and took out my cedar bundle from the pack I had hauled up with me. I lit the herb and watched as the smoke rose and coiled. There was only the slightest of air currents causing the smoke to go astray.

I did nothing with the cedar except light it. The smell of the smoke was comforting. I did not feel an urge to cleanse myself or set an intention. The presence of the ceremonial embers made the moment feel even more remarkable than it already was.

Closing my eyes, I allowed the feeling of peace and tranquillity wash over me. Experiences like this didn't happen every day. I lived most of my life in the city, rarely catching a sunrise because the business of the day would get ahead of me.

Here I was, on the top of a mountain, overlooking two beautiful lakes, facing a stunning and vibrant sky. It was bliss.

I looked down at the lake below me. I could see the shores clearly and I was content to find that I was still alone. Standing up, I stretched my arms toward the sky and looked around. *No one is here.* The high from my hike must have gone to my head because what I did next surprised even myself.

I peeled off my jacket and placed it on the rock beside my adventure pack. The next layers of clothing shed themselves swiftly and suddenly I was standing on a rock, in a place that had been teeming with people the day before, naked.

Feeling the lightest breeze graze my bare skin, I shivered. The brisk morning air was enlivening.

Freedom. True, and unadulterated.

It was a rush to be so shameless, so audacious, so unnerved.

I spread my arms wide and smiled at the rising sun.

As the chill of the morning caused fine hairs to stand, I wondered who would stand for me if not myself.

Breakup Words

NO ONE SAW ME that day. Rigs and I were halfway down the mountain before we saw the first set of hikers climbing up to the lakes. I drove us home and promptly went to bed, falling asleep quickly and snoozing until the early afternoon.

I nearly missed my appointment to donate blood. I woke up startled, looking at the time and realizing there were only a few minutes to spare before I would be late.

I got up, still clothed from my hike, and grabbed my keys.

Rigs was confused by my sudden actions and was at my heels at the base of the stairs.

"You stay," I told him.

He raised a paw to the first step.

"You stay," I said more firmly as I climbed the stairs and shut the door.

I could hear Riggley whine but had no time to settle him.

I made it to the clinic a minute late.

When I walked into the clinic, the receptionist greeted me with a smile. After checking me in, she waved me over to a little booth where a nurse pricked my finger, did a quick blood test, and gave me a form to fill out. It was a questionnaire, and the clinic asked some highly personal questions on it. There was a question on the form which asked if I had been intimate with someone who had been using illegal substances.

Jordan had started taking testosterone to build more muscle at the gym. Testosterone was a controlled substance and Jordan was getting it goodness knows where. As it was technically a true statement, I answered yes. I always did my best to answer the questions honestly.

I had filled out the same questionnaire once before when I donated at another clinic during my last appointment. When I got to the nurse who reviewed my answers, she needed more information. I had texted Jordan questions to clarify whether I was able to donate.

While the previous nurse had looked into the responses I gave and determined it safe to proceed, this nurse checked her resources but came to a different conclusion.

The time before I had been approved to donate, but this time the nurse put a twelve month deferral on me. I wouldn't be able to donate blood for another year.

I walked out of the clinic shocked and frustrated, my thumbs furiously typing out a text to Jordan, hoping for sympathy.

> I just went to donate blood and they put a deferral on me! I can't donate again for another year!

I began walking back to my car when I got his text back.

> Why can't you donate?

I waited to reply until I was sitting in my vehicle.

> Because I answered the questions honestly but she didn't look into their procedure manual like last time. It's because of your steroids.

The next message was jarring.

> WHY DID YOU TELL THEM THAT!?

I was surprised by the all caps. I wrote back, somewhat confused.

> Because the questionnaire asked it? And it was fine last time... I wonder if they could reverse it.

I looked out the window as I waited for the next message. I wasn't about to drive in the middle of this conversation.

> Hallie, I know people who work at that clinic! You KNEW that. Why would you tell them I'm on T?

I paused. We had gone to donate blood together almost a year ago at this clinic and he had mentioned that. He wasn't taking the hormones yet, so he had been able to donate with me.

The questionnaire was supposed to be confidential. They even took me into a private little room to follow up with the questions I had answered. It was a middle-aged nurse and most of the people Jordan pointed out that he knew were young guys on the floor actually taking the blood. I didn't see how any of this information would get back to them.

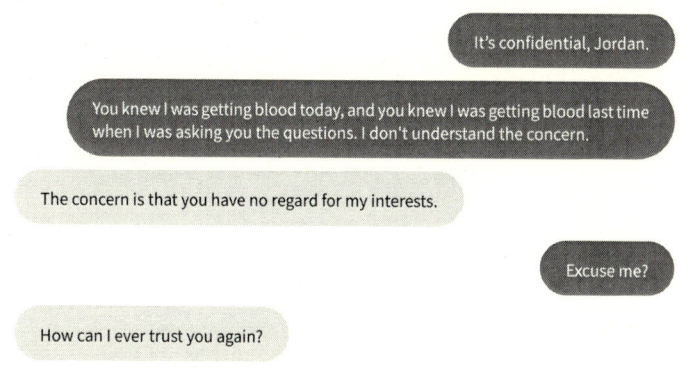

> It's confidential, Jordan.

> You knew I was getting blood today, and you knew I was getting blood last time when I was asking you the questions. I don't understand the concern.

> The concern is that you have no regard for my interests.

> Excuse me?

> How can I ever trust you again?

Too far. Last time he had been helpful when I had come across this situation and this time he was offended by it. I didn't see his point. I had done the right thing by being honest with the responses even if the nurse wasn't right to defer me. I was in a sour spirit over the situation already and this was escalating my irritation.

> Do you really want to go there?

> You betrayed my trust, Hallie. I can't believe you would do that to me!

Betrayed his trust? For being honest in a medical questionnaire that could affect someone's life?

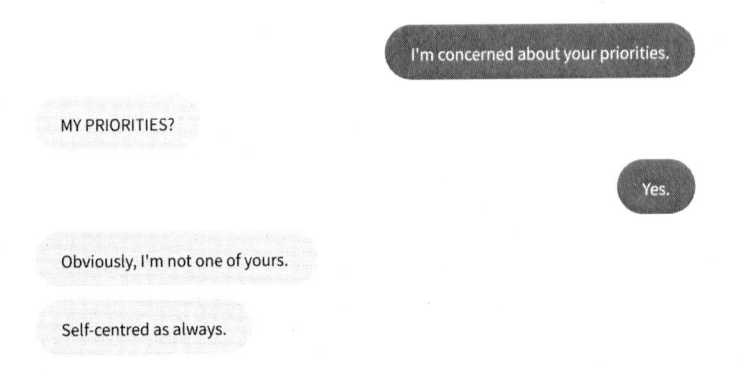

> I'm concerned about your priorities.

MY PRIORITIES?

> Yes.

Obviously, I'm not one of yours.

Self-centred as always.

His text hit a big nerve. It was the steak all over again. I was done with the sarcastic hits that were meant to sting.

Suddenly my last month caught up to me. The uncertainty, the promise of something better.

My thumbs worked faster than my desire to repair our relationship.

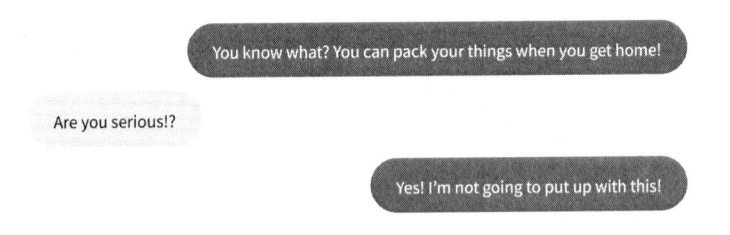

> You know what? You can pack your things when you get home!

Are you serious!?

> Yes! I'm not going to put up with this!

I let out a big breath as I put my key in the ignition and turned my car on. I turned my phone off. My hands were shaking, I was so mad at him. I texted him looking for sympathy and received a response I didn't expect.

The way home was fortunately on a route I took often. My mind was not focused on the road. As I got out of the car, I could hear Riggley howling in the house.

I wasn't thinking as I rushed toward the door. My anger with Jordan was running hot in my veins.

Riggley must have heard my steps because as I opened the door he was right there on the landing.

"YOU GET DOWN! YOU GET DOWN RIGHT NOW." I yelled at him senselessly as I chased him down the stairs.

He cowered as he made it to the base of the stairs. It was as though he thought I would hit him. For a moment, I was so charged from my day I thought that I might.

It wasn't Riggley's fault, though. It wasn't his fault I had been in a rush when I left. It wasn't his fault his dad had triggered my frustration. It wasn't his fault at all.

I crumbled onto the floor crying, reaching out to my shadow, whispering apologies as tears began to prick in my eyes.

Riggley hesitantly came to me and settled into my lap.

We sat like that for quite a while as I cried tears of grief that had been in my heart for months. This was it. I had asked Jordan to leave.

I turned my phone on to see several messages from Jordan which I cleared from my screen, deciding that I was too angry to look at them.

There was another text waiting for me from Danielle.

> Is everything okay?

She knew I would never scream at Rigs like that.

> No, it's not.

I texted back, not looking for sympathy but being honest.

> Come up?

Letting out a big sigh, I got up and pet Riggley behind the ears to let him know I wasn't mad at him.

"Come on, Buddy. We're going upstairs," I said gently.

I still had my shoes on and asked Rigs to be a good boy for our door routine.

He stayed at the bottom this time and came up after I released him. I didn't bother with a leash as he knew the way.

I walked through the gate, around the corner, up the steps, and through the door without knocking.

Riggley followed at my side, his footsteps becoming clicks on the tile of my neighbour's home.

"Hey!" Danielle called from the living room as she rounded the corner to the entry.

My eyes must have given me away because she called, "Fable, Brook, come give Hallie a hug."

"Hallie!" I heard from the back bedrooms with little pattering footsteps to follow.

Fable was the first to arrive, with her sister close on her heels.

She paused, also looking at me. "Are you sad?"

I knelt down behind Riggley, avoiding the swishes of his tail.

"A little, Hunnie."

She slowly squished around Rigs in their small entry and lifted her arms to offer a hug. I pulled her in and held her gently in my arms, leaning my head on her small shoulder and feeling into the embrace.

Brook was playing with Riggley's tongue as he tried to lick her hands.

I let out a half-hearted giggle as I released Fable.

"Why don't you stay for a little and watch some cartoons with the girls?" Danielle asked.

"Cartoons?" Brook asked, jumping little tippy-taps on the spot.

I untangled myself from Fable and stood up, feeling grateful for the opportunity to regulate how I was feeling. "Sure."

Fable took my hand and led me to the living room. Brook took hold of my other hand as we passed and joined us on the couch. Rigs left to explore the kitchen, looking for crumbs.

I lay horizontally on their L-shaped brown chaise and let the girls find their spots to snuggle in. Riggley returned from the kitchen to settled at my feet.

We had done this many times, usually in the early morning when I would come up to babysit when Danielle had a work event and Phillip worked overtime.

Danielle usually attempted to barter with me to pay more for my time, but I rarely gave her a number and would affirm that time shared with her children was enough for me.

It was.

As Fable handed me the remote and Brook curled her little hand into my collarbone, I could feel myself relax.

I didn't ask what they wanted to watch, knowing their favourites already.

After selecting *The Animal Show*, I nestled myself into the cocoon created by my most beloved souls and closed my eyes.

This was what community meant to me. This was so precious, so vibrant, so supportive, so authentic. I felt rich in chosen family. Nicole, Maxille, Danielle, Brook, and Fable—even Phillip.

I was surrounded by a small network I felt loved by.

Jordan loved me, but it was different. This love I felt by my network was genuine, selfless, and reciprocal. Jordan's love felt possessive, conditional, requited.

Every time he made an extravagant dinner, it seemed the expectation of my turn to cook would provide a meal of equal effort and quality. I considered this unobtainable. I lacked the skills, interest, and desired dedication of time to impress him. His expectations were in my actions. He wanted me to rise to his standard of service.

Perhaps he felt the same toward me. I expected him to attempt the effort and quality I held as a standard in my verbiage and tone, and maybe he felt lacking in the same. My hopes for our future were in his emotional availability. I wanted him to rise to a healthy style of communication.

If I felt overwhelmed and uncaring due to his expectations, maybe he felt the same way by mine.

The Animal Show was in the middle of a song about the savanna. I listened to the characters sing about the power of a lion's pride as I drifted between my thoughts and the present moment.

Brook sighed against my chest and Fable was nearly laying on top of me.

This.

Brook's breath whispered against my skin. The rise and fall of Fable's chest matched with mine. I could feel my nervous system calming, my anger subsiding, gratitude replacing it.

When the episode ended, small shifts of movement from both girls let me know it was time to get up.

I kissed the top of Brook's forehead "You girls want to go play?" Neither answered. Fable rubbed her eyes, Brook was blinking, looking like we all had gotten a little rest.

We stayed like that for another moment before Danille came into the living room.

"Dinnertime, girls," she said softly. "Hallie, I made a little extra if you would like to stay. Phillip should be home shortly."

I gingerly began shifting into an upright position, the girls slowly detaching themselves from me.

Riggley lifted his head, his nose sniffing the scent of dinner. Fable was off the couch and wandering over to the table. Brook was still a bit slow to mobilize so I lifted her into my arms, letting her hands encircle the back of my neck.

"Dinner, Hunnie," I whispered in her ear.

A soft cry came from below my chin. She hated dinnertime.

"It's okay, I'll stay with you." I said as I moved to the dining room and set her down in her boosted seat.

She gripped tighter when I tried to release her.

"I'm not going anywhere, I'm just going to sit right beside you." I murmured, removing her hands from behind my head.

"WHO LET THE DOG IN?" I heard from the entry.

"Hallie and Riggley are staying for dinner," Dani told Phillip as I started strapping Brook into the seat. She already had tears falling and looked helpless.

"Well, I guess that's okay." Phillip passed us to go into the bedroom and change out of his dusty attire.

Danielle brought out a folding chair and placed it behind me at the end of the table.

"I want to sit by Hallie, too!" Fable took the seat across from her sister, being tall enough to take an adult chair.

I sat down, with Riggley coming to rest his head in my lap on Fables side of the table. She pet his back, and I gave him soft pets behind his ears telling him, "You'll get dinner soon."

As if he understood, Rigs left to lay at the entry.

Danielle brought two plates for the girls with grilled cheese on them, Brook's cut up into smaller bites and Fable's cut on a diagonal with no crust in sight. A little pool of ketchup garnished each plate.

Phillip returned from the bedrooms and got his plate from the kitchen as Dani brought ours over also.

"It's nothing special," she said as she placed a plate of quinoa pilaf, Brussel sprouts and shredded barbeque chicken down in front of me.

"It's appreciated," I said sincerely as I looked up at her and smiled. "Thanks for being a safe space."

"I've got you, girl." She returned a grin and sat down beside Fable who was nearly finished her first half of the sandwich.

Brook, however, was picking at her pieces, moving them into a line.

I didn't dare rush her, knowing she had a system needing to be honoured before she would eat.

Phillip carried most of the conversation, talking about a new project he was working on and the challenges of his clientele.

Brook's masterpiece was now a perfect circle, and I was nearly done my quinoa.

She looked up at me and I grinned at her. "What shape is that?"

"A sun!" She interpreted my words in her own way.

"Does it have sun rays?" I asked.

She looked at her circle and began removing every third piece of bread and cheese to form a new ring, then tightening the other squares to a smaller circle.

Now some of the pieces were outlier, Brook began arranging the sun rays perfectly, casting out the exiles into the corner of her plate.

Once her sun was to her liking, she started to eat the excess grilled cheese.

I looked over to Dani who seemed to sigh in relief.

This was the battle of dinnertime.

Brook wouldn't eat a bite unless the fare didn't fit her creation.

When all her discards were consumed, she started arranging the meal into a new pattern.

Everyone at the table finished their meal, and Fable excused herself politely to sit down with Riggley and pet him.

I stayed with Brook, encouraging new ways of excluding bites until we were at the final two.

"What's this one?" I asked her, pointing to one.

"You!" she said.

"What's the other one?"

"Your boyfriend..." she trailed.

"Why?" I asked, wondering what she had noticed and how her little mind was perceiving my world.

"You have to eat him." She looked up at me.

"Eat him?" My pitch rose in surprise.

She nodded and lifted the grilled cheese representing Jordan.

After all the surfaced anger from earlier today, I deemed it symbolically necessary to, indeed, eat him.

I chomped on the offered grilled cheese straight out of Brook's little hand, making her laugh.

"Are you going to eat me now?" I mumbled around my bite.

She could not have been faster to pick up the last piece and put it in her mouth, gleaming with accomplishment.

"That's all of them! Good job, Hunnie!" I praised.

I got up and undid the straps keeping Brook secure in her booster. She squirmed down onto the floor.

I let her go join her sister who was now playing tug-of-war with Riggley in the living room with one of their less loved stuffed animals.

I cleared my plate and Brook's and took them to the sink.

Dani was cleaning up the rest of dinner.

"Is this something I'm going to need to get used to? The yelling?" she asked.

I tucked my chin, feeling bad but knowing her comment was heartfelt. "I hope not."

"I know you love those boys, but they are taking more from you than I think you realize." Her words hit home as Riggley came to my side.

Training him had taken quite the toll of patience and I thought I had been weathering it well, but today was a stark exception.

I didn't want to tell her the new finality of my relationship. Didn't want to offer my shifting world yet.

Petting Rigs, I said, "It was my fault today. I left in a rush."

Danielle looked me in the eyes. "I think we know more of your world than you think we do."

Understanding due to the close proximity her comment likely held truth, I replied, "I just want to do better."

"I know you do, and I don't want to pressure you into anything. I just want to see you happy." Danielle passed me some utensils to put into the dishwasher.

I shifted Riggley out of the way to help with the cleanup. He walked away to search under the table for left behinds.

I helped Danielle in silence, contemplating.

After all the dishes were put away, I went to hug the girls who were on the couch with Phillip, watching another episode of *The Animal Show*.

"Are you going home?" Fable asked as I kissed the top of Brook's head goodbye over the ledge of the couch.

"Yes, Hunnie. It's time for me to go." I said. Fable stood on the couch so I could give her a better hug. "See you again soon."

"Bye." Phillip added his brief farewell as I collected my pup.

"Thanks again, Dani," I offered as I put my shoes on in the entry.

She nodded to me. "Anytime, Hallie. We love you."

"I love you, too," I replied, meaning it collectively.

Riggley followed me out of the house and down to our suite.

I took a shower and got ready for bed. Jordan called again just as I was crawling under the covers. His image appeared on the call screen as I debated answering or not. I caved. I had been ignoring him all day.

"Hallie!" he said as I picked up the phone. "I can't lose you, talk to me!"

"What is there to say, Jordan? Your reaction today was uncalled for."

"I know I overreacted. I was scared some of the people in the clinic would find out," he said.

"I get that, but you didn't have to talk to me the way you did!"

"I know. Hallie, you're the kindest girl I've ever known, you are so beautiful, smart, funny, and wise. I couldn't imagine being with anyone else but you. Please don't do this."

Tears came to my eyes because I was still upset with him. I didn't respond.

"Hallie, I love you so much. Please talk to me."

"I'm mad," I said honestly.

"I know, Hallie. Just please. I'll come home tomorrow and I'll do my best not to talk to you like that again."

A big sigh rushed out of my lungs. I was at my wit's end with these arguments and this one had pushed me beyond another threshold. Accusing me of being untrustworthy after I had just suffered the consequence of being honest felt unfair and unjustified.

"I can't keep doing this with you, Jordan. I had to be honest at the clinic because that's what I believe in. If you don't trust me, then this is not a relationship that I want to be in," I told him.

"I trust you. I didn't mean it," he pleaded with me. 'Please, Hallie. Just let me come home."

I didn't say anything. I didn't know what to say.

"I love you so much." His voice wavered, giving away that he was fighting back tears on the other side of the phone.

I paused.

Did I want to end our relationship like this? This was the first time breakup words were spoken since my Journey. In one breath, I wanted it to be over with so that I could move on but in the next, I just wasn't ready. I still loved him. Late at night when I snuggled beside him, I could still imagine a future together. I wanted a future together. The message I received in the Journey had interrupted the long term plans I imagined having with him. My heart was still invested.

I sighed again. "I love you too, Jordan. I just need things to change."

"We'll get through this, Hallie. I'll see you at home tomorrow?"

"Okay. I'll see you at home."

I still had tears in my eyes when I hung up the phone. Earlier in the day, I had taken a step toward leaving the relationship and now I had taken my words back. Frustrated with myself, I rolled over and tried to fall asleep.

I woke up in the middle of the night. My stomach was in knots. Only a few times in my life has my gut turned on me. I've been blessed with fairly good digestive health and discomfort isn't a common occurrence. I stayed in bed for a little while before the discomfort became intolerable. Eventually, I got up and moved to the floor of the bathroom with a cold cloth on my neck for an hour before returning to my room. There might have been an hour or two caught of closed eyes and calm before the early light of day began to brighten the room.

In the morning I was exhausted but it felt like the discomfort had settled. I sent a text to Jordan, letting him know I wasn't well and otherwise spent the morning and early afternoon doing small tasks around the house, taking a nap around midday. By the time I woke up, Jordan was home. I hadn't heard him come in.

"I made food," he said as I came into the kitchen. Pasta was cooking on the stove. "I thought it would make you feel better."

I walked past him to sit on the couch. My tummy had relaxed as I napped and was feeling better, but the sensation remained present.

"Thanks for starting dinner. I don't know how hungry I am, though," I said. "I'm not sure if it's kind of like the flu but maybe I should just have something light like soup."

His face fell ever so slightly as he brought me water and told me to drink it.

"You should at least stay hydrated." He handed me the glass and turned on the TV.

I grabbed a blanket off the edge of the couch and curled up under it, tucking myself into a little ball in the corner. I wondered what the matter was. I wasn't due for my period and cramps rarely last so long. I had forgotten about it for most of the day, but there was still a dull ache which hadn't passed yet. The sensation had become more notable since I had woken from my nap.

I let Jordan finish making supper as I looked through my Social Media.

"Are you feeling okay?" he asked as he sat down beside me. I shifted to nestle my head into the crook of his neck.

"Just uncomfortable," I said.

"Please eat." Jordan pushed. "I know you don't want to and it might not help the feeling, but you really should feed yourself."

He put a plate of pasta and salad in front of me.

"I don't feel like I should..." I replied. The pasta looked amazing. There were cherry tomatoes, spinach, and peppers in a basil pesto and garlic sauce.

I would have been excited for such a meal when I felt like myself, but my appetite wasn't so impressed by it today.

I wasn't sure what was going on with my tummy ache. It wasn't going away. Jordan put in the effort to make something for me, and I didn't want to be ungrateful.

I took a bite of the food in front of me to show my gratitude. It was delicious. The pesto was creamy and fragrant with basil and black pepper. I had a few more bites and then pushed it away, feeling nauseous.

Jordan reached over for the remote and flicked through to our streaming app. He finished his own dinner and then shifted closer so I could snuggle into him.

We watched a few episodes of our favourite show before I was ready for bed. I wasn't paying attention anymore. My head was resting on his chest with eyes closed, trying to ignore the sensations of my body.

I pushed myself up and stretched my arms.

"How are you feeling?" Jordan asked.

I pressed my palms to my eyes as I shifted through gentle motions. "Same. Maybe worse."

"Is there anything I can do?" he offered, taking one of my hands from my eyes to kiss it.

"I don't think so," I said. "I think I just need to wait for this to pass. I'm going to take a shower and get ready for bed and see how it feels in the morning."

I leaned in close to kiss him on the cheek before stepping off the couch and walking to the bedroom. I gathered my towel, fresh pyjamas, and a pair of slippers so that I would be nice and cozy when I got out of the shower.

I took my time letting the water wash over me. I thought over again the stress of our argument.

Jordan was doing his best to try and make amends and act on his best behaviour, but I didn't think we were going to talk it through. The hot water streaming over my back was soothing.

I sighed, reaching for the face wash. This game of looking out for your own needs but also knowing that life is about being there for one another was so challenging. What do you do when the person you love can't accept the way you're offering affection? How do you bridge that? How do you bridge your needs and theirs when communication is supposed to be the tool to help fix things and yet it's like hammering a nail with the back end of a bottle of soda? Each hit risks an eruption and a significant mess to clean.

I scooped the water over my face, rubbing the leftover mascara out of my eyes. *You can do it*, I told myself. *One day at a time.*

Turning off the water, I grabbed my towel from behind the curtain. I pulled the material tight around my shoulders, containing as much heat as I could. *One day at a time.*

I again tossed and turned all night, my tummy in knots. The ache was becoming intense, and I was shifting around every few minutes to find relief. It was becoming so acute that I finally started to think it wasn't something that would pass. I looked to my phone every thirty minutes or so, drifting between boredom, a genuine attempt to rest, and a settling worry that this could be serious.

I reached over and put my hand on Jordan's shoulder. The room was beginning to brighten with daylight. I rolled closer to him so that I could speak softly in his ear.

"Hey, Love? I'm really not feeling well. I'm going to get up," I said gently.

He stirred for a moment, my words waking him from the fog. I kissed him on the shoulder before rolling to the edge of the bed to sit up. Oh goodness, that was worse. It felt like I was supporting a sandbag with my pelvic floor.

"Do you think we should go to Emerg?" he asked, sitting up.

"I think I need to get it checked out. I'll look at the wait times," I said as I moved to the side of the bed to get my phone.

"No, you get dressed. I'll look." He already had his phone in hand.

I turned behind me to the dresser and pulled out the feel-good fashion of comfort: leggings. I planned to wear them with the knock-off fuzzy boots I'd owned since post-secondary.

"Urgent care is quicker," Jordan said. "It's a forty-minute wait instead of two and a half hours at the hospital."

I didn't think about it. I imagined sitting in one of the tiny little chairs in the waiting rooms curled up and tenderly holding myself together. I was in enough pain now that I could hardly stand straight.

"Let's just get to the urgent care and they'll transfer me if it's serious," I suggested.

Jordan swung his legs over the side of the bed and walked over to me. He wrapped his arms around me and kissed me on the forehead. "Okay, let's go to urgent care. Just give me a little to get ready and we'll go."

Words to the wise: if you have a medical issue beyond a broken bone, a minor infection or you just need to rehydrate after a night of very heavy drinking and you're pretending you have the flu, please go to a hospital instead of a halfway clinic.

I didn't have a traumatic diagnostic experience, but I would have been diagnosed faster at the hospital. They took an x-ray in the centre, then sent me across the city for an ultrasound, then made me return to the urgent care where they gave me the option of accepting that maybe I just needed a laxative or getting a CT scan to rule out appendicitis. When the doctor palpated my stomach, I experienced a sharp pain in my right lower quadrant, a telltale sign of the illness.

I asked for the CT scan.

As we waited, Jordan left to get himself some breakfast. He returned with a coffee and a wrap, and a muffin for me.

"I don't think I can eat that," I told him.

"Are you sure you don't want a bite? It's raspberry lemon," he said.

I laughed. "You picked it up knowing my answer, hey? Now you get a muffin."

He chuckled.

"If you didn't want it, I was going to eat it, yeah." Jordan folded back the wrapper of his breakfast wrap and set his coffee and our muffin on the little tray next to the bed I was sitting in.

A short while later, a nurse came in with a bucket of IV supplies, a gown and a gigantic bottle of water. There were three lines drawn on it in sharpie, dividing the bottle into thirds.

"I'm going to get you to put on a gown after I'm done. You'll need to drink the water over thirty minutes, so every ten minutes you have to drink down to a line," she told me.

Slightly intimidating. She poured some of the water into a cup for me and returned the bottle to the table. I took a large sip, and then another.

The nurse was friendly but took several attempts to slip an IV into the crease of my elbow. She was not successful and called in a second nurse who was able to get an IV into a vein under my forearm. A strange place, I thought, and the second nurse admitted that it might not have been the best place for it. The CT needed a large vein for the injection solution.

I put the gown on after the nurses left and finished the water in my allotted time. A porter came by when I was done to take me to my scan. I was a little embarrassed to be getting wheeled around in a gown, but I knew this was all in my best interest.

"I'll see you when you're out," Jordan told me as he kissed my forehead.

The technician was waiting for me at the door as I arrived. The scanner looked like a large white circle with a table going through the centre. She had me lay on the table with my feet facing the device.

"Can I see your IV? I just need to check it and make sure the contrast solution will go through," the technician said. I offered her my arm.

"Hmm," she said. "This might not work but we'll give it a try."

She hooked my IV up to a clear line and pushed a few buttons on a pump behind me.

A pain shot through my arm like a fiery pressure extending down to my fingers. I looked quickly down at my hand.

"How is that?" she asked.

"Umm. Not nice, but it's okay,"

She looked at my face, reading my expression.

"Let's try the elbow again. This goes in for a minute and if it's already hurting it will be very uncomfortable." She gathered supplies for a new IV.

I appreciated her attention to my comfort.

The tech was swift with her next motions and was able to get the IV into my arm with ease. We both laughed at this, wondering what all the fuss had been about.

"Okay, you're ready to go. Just stay very still while the scan is taking place. The contrast injection will make you feel warm. Don't worry, this is normal," she told me before heading back to the control room.

I closed my eyes and focused on taking even breaths. I was suddenly nervous and wanted my scan to be done correctly. The bed started moving under me toward the scanner. I could hear the tech giving me instructions through a speaker nearby.

"Take a deep breath and hold it, Hallie. You're doing great."

I did as she directed and held my breath after a full inhale.

"Okay, I'm going to run the contrast solution now," I heard over the speaker.

The technician had been correct. I could feel a warmth starting at the IV and spreading into my shoulder. It was quickly a full-body sensation making me feel acutely nauseous.

"How are you doing there, Hallie?" the tech asked.

"I'm feeling a little sick," I said tensely as my head started to spin.

The tech rushed out of the control room with a little cardboard bowl and offered it to me. "Here, you can sit up. We're all done."

I sat up and immediately started to heave.

Nothing came up as I hadn't eaten more than a few bites of dinner the night before. Finally, the heaving stopped and I was able to take a breath.

The tech put a hand on my back. "Awe honey, your doctor will come and talk to you about the results, but it was good that we got the scan."

The scan returned positive for appendicitis.

I sent Jordan home, asking him to prepare an overnight bag for me as I was being transferred to the hospital for surgery. He gave me a kiss on the head and promised he would be back before my procedure.

He didn't make it.

I was transferred in an ambulance, met new doctors at the hospital, and then was quickly taken upstairs to the OR.

My anxiety rose the moment I entered the operating room. I felt like I had gone into autopilot.

"Can you tell me your name and date of birth?" a nurse asked me.

I mumbled my details.

The nurse nodded and asked me to transfer from the wheelchair I had been brought up in to the operating table.

I did as I was told, now becoming aware that I was about to be induced into the halfway point between life and death, aware that I could go either direction, aware I was more likely to wake up back to reality, less one piece of my body I no longer needed.

My upper back was now bare against the cold table beneath me and the room was swirling with nurses who were preparing for my procedure. An arterial line was put into my wrist as the IV the CT tech had put in wasn't a direct line, they said.

Once I had a moment of solitude amongst the seemingly chaotic environment, I started to pray.

Spirit, I ask to be protected while I am not in my body. I ask to be cared for and kept safe. May anything toxic or stuck in my relationship be sent out with my toxic appendix. I ask that all negative feelings toward Jordan be sent out, too.

It was a last-ditch effort. A piece of me was going to physically be taken out of my body and I intuitively hoped I could send some emotional energy out with it.

"Hallie, we're going to start now, just take a few deep breaths."

The anesthetist put a mask over my face. I felt warmth in my lower abdomen.

As I breathed in the gas to put me to sleep, I began to feel calm.

Everything will be okay. Everything will be okay. Everything will be okay.

Red room
Red tent
Salt gives orange glow
Sun is setting
Spring leaves drift with the breeze
Blue sky standing by
Waiting for the dark of night
The reflecting moon which follows

Blocking of One's Path

I WOKE UP FROM the procedure in a dark little hospital bed in the middle of the night. Nothing hurt yet. I was a little disoriented but otherwise felt fine. I lifted my gown to see what had happened to me. I had three little incisions on my tummy. They were covered in strips of tape. I lay back down and promptly fell asleep.

When I woke up, Jordan was there. "How are you feeling?"

"Not too bad, actually," I told him. I was still a little dazed. It was probably the drugs. I allowed Jordan to sit me up so I was upright.

I looked around at the room. There was a window to my right and Jordan had sat back down on a chair beside my bed.

"I'm sorry I missed it," he said, looking at me with a disappointed expression. "They wouldn't let me visit until this morning."

"That's okay," I replied. "I found the strength to do it on my own."

A nurse came in just then and said she needed to get me up. I would be discharged soon as long as I could walk and get my things together.

She helped me walk over to the washroom to get cleaned up and changed out of my hospital gown.

Jordan had packed a bag with some comfortable clothes. After I freshened up, I reached into the pocket where he had stored my socks. The tips of my fingers brushed against something cold and hard. I grasped the object and pulled it out. It was my favourite crystal. My heart softened a little. Of course he had packed me something he felt would comfort me. He might not have made it for my operation, but I could only imagine he had been worried about me while I was going through the procedure.

The nurse led me back into the room and we waited until I received discharge papers saying that I could go home, with care instructions for my incisions and a list of things not to do so I could heal properly.

I was amazed it had barely been twenty-four hours since I had walked into the urgent care centre and I was already being sent home, minus one disruptive appendix.

Jordan went to get the car and I was brought to the doors in a wheelchair.

My recovery went pretty well once we were home. I was a little slower and more careful with my movements for the first couple of days but Jordan would take me for walks around the block to get me up and moving. We didn't fight at all. It was lovely.

When I was all healed, Nicole invited me to a Red Tent Ceremony. She was on her way to pick me up and I was waiting on the grass out front.

I had never been to one before, but Nicole told me it was a women's circle where it was safe to talk about life and spirituality. She had attended several gatherings so far and Tony had given her the oracle deck at one of these events.

"Hello, Gorgeous!" Nicole exclaimed from her rolled-down window.

"Hey! Thanks for the ride," I said as I climbed into the compact SUV. My incisions didn't hurt anymore and I was able to get in easily.

"How are you feeling?" Nicole asked as she pulled away from the curb.

I had texted Nicole and called my mother as I was being transferred to the hospital to let them know I was about to go in for surgery.

"I'm feeling really good! I'm shocked this happened to me, but otherwise, I'm doing well," I told her.

"Tell me what happened! I want to hear the story."

I told her about the fight I had with Jordan and how later that night I started to experience discomfort in my tummy. It took about the length of the trip to the ceremony to tell her about my diagnostic experience and how scary it was to go through the operation alone. I was just sharing the prayer I said before I was anesthetized as we pulled up to the little house where the Red Tent was going to take place.

"I think it's perfect that you asked spirit to help you send out the toxic energy in your relationship. I think that's exactly what I would have done, too!" Nicole said as she unbuckled her seatbelt.

We got out of the car and walked up to the house. It wasn't a large home. The steps leading up to the door were framed with pots of newly planted flowers and small decorations were hanging from the tree which sat in the centre of the yard. I looked up at the branches and saw a stained glass bird spinning gently in the light breeze.

We rang the doorbell and waited, hearing footsteps getting louder as someone came to answer the door.

"Tony!" Nicole chimed as the door opened. "How are you?"

A small woman stood smiling at us. She had dreadlocks concealed by a light pink bandana and was wearing natural materials. There were gentle lines of aging around her eyes and kind-looking features shaping her face.

"Nicole, my sweet girl, I am doing well! You've brought a friend this time, too! Please come in!" Tony opened the door wider for us.

I smiled and introduced myself as we walked into the entryway to take off our shoes. "I'm Hallie. I've heard so much about you from Nicole!"

"Nicole has shared a little about you also, so it's nice to finally put a name to a face," Tony said. She waved us up a little flight of stairs into the living room.

There were red cushions scattered on the floor and red sheets hanging from the walls. In the centre of the room a red circular rug with candles, malas, and crystals in the middle of it acted as an altar. Two women were sitting on the couch chatting. I smiled at them as we walked through the living room and into the kitchen. A few more women were standing around the island. One of the ladies poured a cup of tea from a teapot. She looked up at Nicole and I.

"Welcome! Would you two like a cup?" she asked.

"Yes, please!" we responded in unison.

Nicole knew a few of these women already and made introductions for me as we moved around the island with steaming hot cups of chai masala. There were only a handful of people to meet and all of them were friendly and welcoming.

The lady who poured us tea was just a little older than Nicole and I. Thick auburn hair reached her mid-back and her green eyes were kind yet held an intensity that was difficult to pinpoint. The emerald shirt she wore was a complement to her features. She introduced herself as Andrea.

"Have you drawn an item yet tonight?" Her green gaze looked over to the table where there was a box covered with black cloth. "Reach in and take whatever touches your hand. It will be your talisman for the night."

"Oooh," Nicole said, moving toward the box. She lifted the cloth while looking at me over her shoulder, her other hand reaching into the box. She smiled as she discovered her talisman and drew her hand out. A feather was pinched between her fingers.

"Oooh!" she said again. "A feather!"

It was from a magpie. I could see white in the centre and iridescent reds, greens, and blues along the black. It was lovely. Nicole looked at me expectantly and nodded her head toward the box. "Your turn!"

I walked over to the table and reached for the cloth. It was soft like silk but it didn't shimmer in the light. I looked Nicole in the eye as I lowered my hand into the box. My fingertip grazed something spongy and I withdrew my hand slightly, startled.

"Ah!" I exclaimed. "There could be anything in here!"

The women in the kitchen were laughing with me as I lowered my hand again. I let my fingers graze over several shapes and textures before I settled on something that I could tell was quite small. I lifted my hand to see what I had acquired.

A toy building block. I giggled, remembering playing with them in my childhood. This one was a block of six and it was blue. I liked it. I smiled, holding it up for Nicole to see. "Look!"

She laughed. "Very nice."

Tony walked into the kitchen and announced that the ceremony would be starting. I picked up my cup of tea and held it with my talisman as I followed Nicole and the other ladies into the living room. Some sat on couches and others took a seat on the cushions. I liked the look of one of the cushions and sat down next to Nicole. I put my cup of tea and my toy block down on the ground in front of me.

Tony dimmed the lights in the room and lit candles. The ambiance became cozy and inviting. A couple of the women were speaking in hushed voices until Tony took her seat in the circle.

"Good evening, sacred souls," she began. "This evening we gather as sisters to work through the big and heavy circumstances we are encountering in our worlds."

Tony moved to grab something from the centre of the altar we had formed a circle around. She lifted a driftwood stick draped with small strips of red cloth in a mix of different textiles.

"We pass this stick among us and whoever holds it will have an audience from the rest. This stick has been passed around many times through many ceremonies and it is a tradition that new sisters tie a strip of cloth to the speaking stick." Tony looked at me. She reached forward again and lifted a strip of red lace, passing it to the woman on her left. "Please give this to our new sister, Hallie. She will tie the strip onto the stick when it is given to her."

In a combined effort from the women in the circle, the strip of lace made it into my hands. It was delicate and feminine. I held it in my lap as Tony continued to speak.

"It is up to you how much you would like to share with us, but please know that this is a safe space to say what is on your heart." Tony's voice was soft and comforting.

I looked at Nicole and she smiled at me, nodding gently. I read her body language and knew she had brought me to this women's circle so I could continue seeking peace and reassurance in my quest to honour the message I received in my Shamanic Journey. She offered support by her invitation, and I could feel the warmth of appreciation bloom in my chest.

"Who would like to begin?" Tony asked, looking around the circle.

A woman who appeared more mature than the rest of us raised her hand. There were streaks of white and grey in her hairline and she sat with a regal posture. The stick was passed through two sets of hands before it arrived at the speaker. The woman introduced herself and, after a pause, began to share her story.

"Someone from my past has reappeared in my present," she said, speaking with a gentle cadence, her voice easily carrying through the circle. "I've carried the heartache of them for years and now old memories are surfacing."

Her eyes were glistening with tears that didn't fall. It was obvious this was dear to her heart. "I must address the feelings I have for them today, though I admit there is some confusion between fondness and pain."

She passed the stick to Tony who placed it on the floor in front of her. Tony put a hand over her heart and sat with a silent gaze toward the woman. I could feel the love and support being offered by this gesture. After a moment, Tony spoke. "Thank you, sister, for sharing with us. Are you open to receiving support?"

"Yes, I am," the woman said.

Tony lifted the stick and looked toward the circle. 'Does anyone have any guidance to share? Any support to offer? Any love to give?"

Nicole put up her hand. The stick was passed around the circle until it reached her. She smiled at the woman with the grey hair.

"It can be tough to feel contradictory emotions toward someone," Nicole spoke kindly. "I had this happen, too, with someone from high school. They had hurt me deeply with their actions and reached out to me last year to make amends.

"The resurfacing of old feelings affected my life for a month or two, but eventually, they faded. I moved on and enjoyed my life again." Nicole told the woman, "I hope you can feel this way soon, too."

The woman nodded and put her hand over her heart just like Tony had, smiling at Nicole. It was a respectful gesture that conveyed an honouring of the other person's words. It seemed to be a part of the culture of this gathering to give this gesture after sharing. The motion was warming and kind.

Tony spoke again, "Does anyone else have words to share?"

She looked around the circle at the women sitting quietly. None of them raised their hands. "Would our new member like to go next? Hallie, do you have a story in need of release?"

I looked at Nicole. She smiled at me and offered the clothed piece of wood. I accepted the stick and held it in my lap, lifting the strip of lace.

The driftwood branch was twisted and snarled in only the way water could bend such a thing. It was smooth to the touch in the places that were bare.

I selected an area in the middle of the stick to tie my fabric. I gently wrapped the lace and tied it tight so the ends were free like the other strips of cloth. When I was done, I kept my eyes on the piece of driftwood, searching for the right words to say.

I sighed. "My name is Hallie, and I've been enduring an internal war about a message I received during a Shamanic Journey. The message told me that I needed to be alone to grow, and right now I have a boyfriend. I think we need to break up because our relationship isn't healthy, but I care about him so much that I'm finding it a challenge. I love him, and this has been so hard.

"I want to do the right thing, and I don't want to hurt him, but I do want to honour my inner voice. I feel like this is important, but it's also intimidating to not know what I'm giving this relationship up for." I took a glance around the circle as the women looked back at me with interest. I wasn't sure what else there was to say without feeling like I was talking too much. I was still holding the driftwood stick, though, so I had the freedom to say anything. I took a deep breath.

"We got into a fight, but this one was different. I told him I wanted to break up and then I took it back. I ended up getting appendicitis the same night and I can't help but think The Universe was sending me another message. I'm having trouble finding peace, as I've been uncertain whether this is the right decision. I'm open to guidance, and I welcome words of wisdom." I spoke from my heart and felt better after it was off my chest. I passed the stick back to Tony, who had a look of curiosity in her eyes as she gazed at me. She put a hand on her heart and nodded at me before turning her attention back to the circle.

"Does anyone have any wisdom to offer Hallie?"

A hand raised across the circle from me. It was the woman who had poured us tea, Andrea.

Tony passed the stick and then got up and moved to a bookshelf behind us. Andrea waited until Tony was finished grabbing a book from the shelf and resumed her seat before she spoke.

"This might not seem relatable, but I think it will help," she started. "When I was dating my partner, I experienced a period of uncertainty. I loved him so much, but we were at the point in our relationship where we needed to decide if we were going to build a future together or let each other go. I wasn't happy with the way things were going and I needed something to change.

"My solution was to form an ultimatum. I felt like he wasn't taking our future seriously and I needed him to quit the dead-end job he'd had since he was a teenager and find something more mature or choose to go to school. If he didn't, I would have walked away from the relationship. I gave him six months and a lot of encouragement. Within two months he found a new job and enrolled in classes to become a tradesman! He took me seriously when I told him what I needed to be able to build a stable future with him and now four years later, we're married.

"Where I'm going with this, is I was at a crossroads. I didn't know whether to take a step forward or a step back but I knew I needed to choose. I got clear on what my needs were to make things work with my partner and I put it in the hands of The Universe. He would step up to the plate or he wouldn't, and that would make my decision for me.

"It seems like you are at this same point as I was all those years ago. You love him, but maybe something is missing in your relationship that you need to feel like you can stay in it. Who knows, maybe The Universe recognizes something needs to shift and is making you uncomfortable because it doesn't want you to settle for less than you deserve. The Universe works in mysterious ways, and I hope it brings you peace after all is said and done. I'm sending you love and support to get through this."

Andrea spoke kindly and sincerely. I put my hand on my heart like I had seen the other women do in thanks for her offering to me.

After a moment, Tony put her hands up to ask for the stick back, and Andrea returned it to her. "I have something I believe might help also, Hallie."

Tony had the book she retrieved from the shelf laying open in her lap. I hadn't noticed her flipping through the book as Andrea had been speaking but it seemed as though Tony found the page she was looking for.

"This book has helped me to understand the spiritual significance of illnesses I have endured. Illness can be a manifestation of our emotional environment. Experiences that influence our spirit positively or negatively can also affect our health. Would you like to see what it says for appendicitis?" Tony asked.

I nodded. "What does it say?"

"*Fear of the unknown. Blocking of one's path,*" she said. "Does that resonate with you?"

It did. My biggest fear of going through with the separation was what value it would have on my future. I didn't want to be making a mistake and losing out on the most significant relationship I'd ever had.

"Yes, I'm terrified of not knowing what comes next. I can't believe it says I blocked my path, that's so weird." Tony didn't pass the stick to me, but I answered her question anyway.

"Take a look at the talisman you picked tonight," Tony told me.

I looked down. I laughed, assessing my selected talisman. "It's a block!"

"*That's* so weird," said Tony. There were giggles around the circle.

I picked up the little block and held it in my hands. The accuracy of the book scared me a little. If I got appendicitis just because I took one step forward, and another step back, then I was afraid of what The Universe would do to me if I didn't listen up.

I looked up to Tony and put my hand over my heart again. I mouthed the words "*Thank you.*"

Tony nodded and then turned her attention to the circle. "Does anyone else have words to share or support to give?"

No one else raised their hands so Tony moved on.

More stories were told by the women in the circle. Many of them were concerned about relationships or career choices. I listened intently, feeling comforted that my problems were just as big as anyone else's. Tony consulted another book or two as a resource and the other women were all so supportive to one another.

Nicole humbly passed her turn to speak but was a source of guidance for a few of the women. I was always so proud of her ability to be of service and still seemingly have it 'all together'. She was my rock when I needed support and she thrived in environments where she could help others. This was one of the many qualities about her which made me appreciate having her as a friend.

Tony closed the circle with a meditation, focusing on our solar plexus chakra. "Oftentimes, we will focus our attention on the heart chakra and work to open or heal it, but we do not pay attention to the surrounding chakras which must also be open in order for this energy to flow. The solar plexus chakra is important because this is where we draw our personal power from in order to take action in our lives."

She instructed us to visualize yellow light flowing a foot in front of our navel as we breathed in, and then sweeping back a foot behind our navel as we breathed out. This pulsing of light was supposed to help clear blockages and reset the chakra.

I felt good after the circle closed. All of us gathered in the kitchen again to talk and to give hugs before slowly trickling out the door. I approached Andrea before she left to say thank you for sharing her story with me. "I appreciated your support in the circle. I've been so torn over acting in the fairest way to move forward with this and your words helped a lot."

"You're welcome, Hallie. I know you'll have your own way of approaching this which will likely be different than mine, but I wanted to share what I needed to do to get out of my situation of feeling stuck and immobile. I also had The Universe giving me messages at the time, so I can relate to what you're going through. I just didn't want you to feel like you had no power in this situation. You *always* have free will, no matter what The Universe says!" Andrea gave me a lasting hug with an extra squeeze of support.

Andrea moved to grab her coat as Tony approached us. "Thank you, Andrea, for coming and being a guide tonight."

"Of course! I just hope it helped," Andrea replied. "Goodnight, Ladies, I've got to run but I hope you have a great night!"

"Goodnight, Andrea! Take care!" Nicole and I chimed.

We were the last ones left in the kitchen. The rest of the women had already departed for the night and it was just Nicole, Tony, and myself.

"Nicole had spoken about you at our last meeting," Tony said, looking at Nicole and then shifting her attention to me. "I'm glad you were able to attend tonight, and I'm glad we were able to meet."

"Me too," I replied with a smile. "This was so helpful. I can't believe how accurate your book was!"

"The Universe works in mysterious ways, but rarely is it wrong."

Nicole and I gave hugs and said goodbye.

As Nicole dropped me off at my house she said, "You can do this, Hallie. You're braver than you think and The Universe has something waiting for you. You just need to trust it."

Trusting wasn't my forte. I wondered if I would be able to let go enough to make room for the promised future I knew was on the horizon.

A Cosmic Ultimatum

In my heart, I knew my intuition had told me a message I needed to hear. I still had free will, however, and a part of me still wanted to believe that we could make it work. I continued to feel that maybe there was a broken part of myself that I needed to heal so that I could step up and be the partner Jordan had been asking me to be. I knew there were two options in front of me and I didn't think I could leave Jordan without feeling guilty, or feeling that I had left because I wasn't willing to put in the work.

Taking Andrea's story to heart, I made a decision that I felt would allow me to be at peace moving forward. I decided that I wanted to meet Jordan at his best. I needed to hear that there were things that he liked about himself. I needed to know that he could acknowledge his value so that I didn't have to do so for him.

I wanted to allow Jordan to do the work that I was asking of him, but I also knew that I would need this to come to a conclusion before I committed to living together again.

My cosmic request: to have Jordan be able to say three things that he liked about himself as our one year lease expired or I would be re-signing it alone.

Coming to this conclusion meant I would need to resume looking for more work soon, which felt like a chore, but if I would need to cover expenses alone, a job would be necessary.

I hated the marketing, the cold-calling. Going to brick and mortar shops and asking how to contact the owner so I could pitch my services. Scrolling social media and trying not to sound like a scam artist when I made a connection.

I loved the work, though, and asked for generous compensation. Working with the brand, creating a story out of their values, and meeting the key players of the team was often an amazing experience. I loved filming, editing, creating.

It was on the night of a full moon when I finally told Jordan I was ready to talk about the night I had come home crying.

"Hey, Love, would you like to go for a walk with me?" I asked after dinner. Jordan nodded and we both put on light jackets, and Jordan grabbed Rigs' leash. As we were putting on our shoes, I could hear vintage tunes coming from upstairs. Danielle's voice could be heard singing along.

Riggley waited until he was released then tromped up to join us.

We stepped out into the cool night air.

As we left the house, I could see Danielle in the kitchen. Brook was in her arms. She must have seen our automatic porch light come on because Dani came to the window and waved as I opened the gate.

I waved back, smiling as Jordan clipped Riggley into his leash.

After closing the gate, I gave an extra wave to let them know we wouldn't be staying to chat.

Brook smiled to her mother and I could see them laughing but heard only the light spattering of rain starting to fall.

"Are you going to be warm enough?" Jordan asked.

Feeling warm and having on a waterproof jacket, I replied, "Yes, I think this is fine."

We walked a little ways before I tentatively asked, "How's work?"

He sighed. "It's doing okay. Things are getting better, and some issues have been resolved."

"That's good." I reached for his free hand as he had Rigs' leash in the other. I still didn't want to pry too much into what those issues were. "I'm glad things are improving."

Jordan seemed much less stressed than he had been over the winter and his outlook was positive. It was refreshing to hear, especially in light of what I was about to tell him.

The rain was a light sprinkle now, with drops hitting my face every few seconds.

When we arrived at the park, Riggley was set free to explore. We walked to my tree and sat down on damp ground. The moon was bright and full in front of us. The park was lit enough to see the shapes of the trees and the features of our surroundings.

This was the perfect moment to tell him about everything I had been experiencing.

"I wanted to talk to you," I began. "Do you remember when I went to the Shamanic Journey class? The one with the drum?"

"Yeah, you were so upset when you came home," Jordan said quietly.

"Well, that's because I received a message that I really didn't want to hear," I told him. "I haven't been ready to share it with you until now."

I told him all about the Journey, about how it felt like every time I thought about him it was like he was out of reach. I told him the message clearly stated I needed to be alone.

"You want to break up?" he asked.

"Jordan, you know I love you. I think that's an impossible choice for me to make, but we've talked about how I've been feeling trapped. The message I received from the Journey was powerful."

He pulled a tissue out of his pocket. I was surprised he had one. "So what now then?"

"I think for these last couple years you've been having a hard time feeling at peace. I want to see you be happy, and I can't give that to you. I believe we need to be able to give happiness to ourselves first. I think I've been feeling stuck because I still sense that somehow you're waiting on me to provide the feeling for you."

"I'm trying to be happy," he said. "And I don't think I'll ever be truly happy without you."

My heart. "I know, Jordan. I think that's the thing. I need you to be happy without me to be happy with me. I think this is a good time to turn over a new leaf and believe things can be better."

Jordan wiped his eyes with the tissue.

"I have something to ask of you. I want to believe we can make it through this but I need something from you so I can keep holding on," I told him.

"What's that?" he asked as he took a deep breath.

I hesitated, needing a moment to centre before I gave my request. "I need you to be able to tell me three things that you like about yourself before I can sign another lease to live with you."

Silence.

A cloud passed in front of the moon.

A deep sigh.

"Okay."

"Okay?" I asked, surprised.

"Yeah," he said. "You're right. I need to do some of this myself."

I felt relief. I let out the breath I was holding in a sigh of my own.

"Thank you," I said. "This has been so hard to figure out and it's not something I want to do but I feel like this is the only way I can keep moving forward."

"I know. I just don't want to lose you," he said, his voice cracking at the end.

"I know, Jordan. I tried my absolute best to find a way for you to keep me," I said as I leaned in to kiss him.

He returned my kiss before pressing against the tree to stand up.

"I love you," he told me, offering me a hand.

I took it. "I love you, too. That's not changing anytime soon."

To me, this request was the whispered password for entrance into the destiny I had yet to discover. To the hush-hush, invitation-only event with a doorway that blended into inconspicuous surroundings, yet led to an experience that would make the heart skip as one walked through the portal.

I had just given him the 'Open Sesame' for my future. It was now up to him to make it to the party.

I wondered if I would be ready for the outcome. If he answered with the password, what promised future would I be parting with to keep him? Would this really be the shift we needed to proceed with a healthier relationship, or had I just given him the key to keep me feeling trapped and unloving?

Pratibha's Path

I PURCHASED TICKETS FOR Nicole to come to the Pratibha Yoga Festival with me for Christmas in anticipation of this spring. We hadn't gone on a trip just the two of us in a few summers and this would be our first whole weekend adventure together in a long time.

We had planned and prepared over the weeks leading up to it, creating our schedules and curating our class preferences. After my Journey brought the allusion to the festival, I was eager to see what inspiration was to come from it.

Nicole picked me up early on the morning of, and we drove for a couple of hours to Banff where the festival was taking place. When we finally pulled into the parking lot of the venue and got out of the car, we were buzzing with excitement.

"I can't believe we're here!" Nicole exclaimed as she walked to the back of the car to get our yoga mats from the trunk.

I rummaged through my purse to find my mala so I could wear it to the opening ceremony. When I finally found it, I lifted it over my head and around my neck. Nicole had made it for me for my last birthday. The beads were made of amethyst and at its base was a little elephant carved out of marble. A small purple tassel hung from the elephant. It was my favourite piece of jewelry.

I got out of the car to help Nicole unload. "I'm excited for the Chakra workshop we have tomorrow!"

"I think that's the one I'm looking forward to the most, too!" she said as she got her bag out of the back of the car and placed it beside her yoga mat which was now leaning beside mine against the vehicle.

When we had everything together and organized, we shut the back of the car and began to walk toward the venue. The parking lot was separated from the venue by a path through the trees. As we walked through the conifers, I looked around at their mossy branches and took in a big, deep breath.

The day was brighter than it had appeared in my Journey, but if I took just a second to stop what I was doing and look at the mountains, the quality of their majesty was the same as it was in my vision.

I needed this. I needed the space to take a break, relax, and come home to myself. I smiled at Nicole. "I'm glad we're here."

Nicole grinned back at me. "Me too, Hun!"

We made it through the small forest to the convention centre. As we walked in the doors, we were greeted by volunteers who guided us to trade in our tickets for wristbands. When we were all checked in, we walked through a small market of shops and vendors to the main practice space.

We walked through tables offering handmade bags for yoga mats, sparkling gemstone bracelets with natural healing properties, and adaptogenic supplements for overall wellness. Textiles, trinkets, tinctures. I had a passing curiosity about what it might be like to be a business offering such wares.

We entered a cavernous room with high ceilings. The space looked industrial with wooden accents in the design of it, giving the room a natural appeal. There were others who had already begun to lay their mats down and prepare for the class. Nicole and I left our bags at the side of the room and took our water bottles and mats with us to find a spot to practice.

The front stage was beautifully decorated, and some activity around it suggested that the class would be starting soon. There were freshly cut log stumps nestled in green ferns. There were soft, twinkly lights wrapped among the greenery, and a few lanterns and Buddha sculptures scattered throughout.

We waited a few more minutes as the room filled with yogis, and the quiet chatter in the room rose a little higher. I looked at my phone to check who the instructor of this class was going to be.

The festival had an app with the schedule on it so it would be easy to see where we were supposed to be throughout the weekend. The opening class said it was supposed to be a 'Spicy Flow' taught by Spencer Hade. She normally taught at a studio in the mountain town.

"Hallie," Nicole whispered, "I think it's about to start!"

The chatter of the room slowly transitioned to the soft beat of music. To the left of the stage I could see a DJ beginning to twist the dials and knobs on his deck. On the stage a small woman was adjusting a microphone. I put my phone face down on silent in front of my mat so it wouldn't distract me.

The small woman stepped onto the centre of the stage and called out to the sea of yogis with a voice that commanded presence.

"Hello and welcome to the Pratibha Yoga Festival! Please make your way into *Samastitihi*, equal standing and we will begin!"

Nicole and I both shifted from our seats into standing, as the rest of the room stood as well.

"As we begin this class, I want all of you to begin thinking about your intention for this weekend. What brought you here? What do you hope to gain from being at this festival? We will write our intentions in ink after this class, but for now, we will move to clear our minds and prepare for reflection."

I already knew my intention for this weekend. I wanted to know the significance behind this festival and why it had come to me in the Shamanic Journey.

"Inhale, raise your arms above your head, exhale, fold at the hips to *Uttanasana*. Inhale, halfway lift, *Ardha Uttanasana*. Exhale jump or step back into *Chaturanga Dandasana*."

I followed Spencer's words and let my body move. I had never heard the Sanskrit words for the poses used in a class before, and I was impressed by her vocabulary. I moved and flowed to the teacher's cues, following the steady cadence of her voice. The pace was quick, and it took some work to keep up.

"Your *Drishti*, or gazing point, is meant to give you a visual centre. How do you stay focused?"

Spencer's voice floated above me as I sat in childs pose and everyone else in the room was in downward dog. We were finishing our fifth consecutive sun and salutation.

The yoga classes I had been to were mostly slow, alignment focused classes. This, was already something else.

I looked over at Nicole, who was also in child's pose. We made eye contact and she mouthed to me "WTF".

I was thinking the same thing myself. It seemed like the rest of the room held downward dog forever. "Exhale, look between the hands to step or jump into *Ardha Uttanasana.*"

I stepped up from childs pose to a half forward fold and eventually met everyone standing tall at the top of our mats in *Samastitihi*. I shook out my arms and found a spot on the stage to stare at. There were at least five hundred people in the room practicing and several volunteers offering assists. An ocean of yogis wearing their best leggings and cutout tops, sporting malas and gemstone bracelets. I tried not to see them.

"Inhale, sweep your arms to the sky, and bend your knees as though you would sit on a chair. *Utkatasana*. Raise your arms to the sky and gaze to your thumbs. This is where you will find stillness," Spencer Hade instructed. I stared at my thumbs. "Exhale, fold. *Uttanasana*. Are you steady yet?"

The poses were challenging for both my body and my mind. "You may take a child's pose if you need it, dear ones, but I promise this practice is worth it. The fire that we are burning is being stoked to align us with something higher, grander, more inspiring than we can understand right now."

I did not take child's pose again. I set my gaze to a point along the stage and I chose to work through the challenge. I felt strong. I felt sturdy. I thought this may possibly have been one of the best classes I had ever taken.

Spencer Hade was a skilled teacher. She spoke with confidence, and her words acknowledged the difficulty of the flow while at the same time inspiring you to power through it. Her message was powerful. Her presence held strength.

We flowed through seemingly every variation of the standing poses and eventually moved to the seated stretches.

"Do not lose focus here. We are seated, and it is restful, but that does not mean our attention must drift." Spencer had been walking around the room since the beginning of the class and just now stepped between Nicole's mat and my own. I could hear her voice beneath the microphone as she spoke. "Inhale, straighten your spine, exhale, fold. Reach your chest forward toward your toes. *Pashchimottanasana.*"

Spencer surprised me by stepping behind me on my mat. She placed her feet on either side of my hips and leaned on my lower back with her shins. I relaxed and let her weight soften me so my nose finally touched my knees.

"Inhale, rise." Spencer let up pressure on my back and continued her path around the room.

She led us through the last of the seated postures, and finally it was time for *Savasana.* "The ancient yogis said that a rigorous yoga practice burns up the Karma within us. That to practice, and to practice fiercely, is to set fire to the inner turmoil which holds us hostage."

I closed my eyes and lay back on my mat. My hands were turned up to the sky. My body felt heavy and weighted, sinking into the earth.

"To endure a challenging practice is to tidy our world within. May you feel clearer now. May you be ready to set your intentions."

Soft beats from the DJ played for a few more minutes as we rested. The calming, tropical sound of a hang drum was harmonious with gentle chanting. I let myself relax and absorb into the floor.

My mind drifted as I rested, thinking of what I had been through since I received my message. I felt confident even though I hadn't separated with Jordan yet; I was still on the right path. I was here. I had made it to the Yoga Festival, and this was supposed to be a place which brought me answers.

I thought back to the last messages under the drum.

A yellow bike on a beach with palm trees. A familiar beach, but I never intended to return.

A steaming mug of chai in a trendy cafe. I loved chai, but had never been to the cafe, full of flowers and floral art on the walls.

The floating whispers of feathers in the wind. They were floating over rocks with blue turquoise beads at the base of black feathers.

The flashing lights of a festival's stage. This could be any stage, at any time. I loved festivals! The lights were red, and white, and orange, and yellow. I could not see anything further.

Two glasses of wine clinking in a vineyard. White wine. The vineyard was leafy, past bloom but before the grapes had formed.

Myself, sitting at the edge of a stream with a set of singing bowls, playing sweet songs for the water. The canopy of trees around me shaded the entire stream. The colours were dull and muted, but the scene, serene and beautiful. The stream looped and coiled, with a bridge in sight nearby.

What did all of this mean?

I sighed. There were times where I felt like I was betraying my intuition by letting this drag out with Jordan. It had been months since my Shamanic Journey, and there were times I wondered why I hadn't just gotten it over with already. I had given Jordan my ultimatum, though, and it was out of my hands now anyway.

"Begin to move your fingers and your toes. Warm up the body and when you're ready, come to a seat."

I stretched and shifted, my head turning to look at Nicole. She still had her eyes closed and was still. I thought she had fallen asleep. As I sat up to a seated position, I brushed her hand. Her eyes fluttered and she began to move.

At the top of my mat was a small amber glass jar with a candle in it. I picked up the candle to look at it. Nicole sat up, blinking and rubbing her eyes. I smiled.

A few volunteers walked around the aisles of mats, passing around golden pens.

"At the top of your mat there should be a candle. We will collectively be setting our intentions for this weekend as our opening for the festival," Spencer called out over the seated yogis. "I want you to tune into the new clarity and let your intentions surface."

I already knew my intention. I just needed one of the golden pens to write it onto the candle. There weren't enough for everyone so I waited patiently until my neighbour was done writing on her amber jar.

Once I had the pen in hand, in the neatest print I could manage on the small, curved surface I wrote the words:

Please reveal the next chapter of my path.

Silently, to myself, I added:

Show me what I am giving up my world for.

The second phrase formed on its own, no less significant than was written on the jar.

Spencer then called for everyone to come up to the stage and place our candles on the wood stumps and around the decorations. Nicole and I walked up to the stage together, let a volunteer light our candles, and placed our amber jars side by side between fir branches.

It was a lovely way to start the weekend.

As agreed, the class Nicole and I were looking forward to the most was a Chakra Reading workshop by a clinic in the area. This class had nearly been full when we went to register for it and we had barely squeezed in on the day registration went live.

When we got to the room where the class was taking place, it was entirely full. Nicole and I had only standing room left at the back of the small space. We respectfully shuffled in front of the crowd, and as we reached a spot near the corner, I stepped behind Nicole to ensure she was able to have a good view of the lecture.

After waiting several minutes and talking with some of the women around us, the teacher finally walked in and took her place at the front of the room. Merenya Rodell was an intelligent-looking woman, tall with long dark hair.

"Hello, everyone! Welcome to Chakra Reading 101," she called out as she looked around the room. "I'm sorry this is such a small space, but we did not expect this class would be so highly desired!"

Merenya introduced herself as a psychosomatic therapist and an osteopath. She worked out of a little clinic in a neighbouring town.

"The chakra's are our energy centres," Merenya began. "They are intimately connected to our subconscious mind. Imbalances in our chakras can manifest in our physical posture and how we carry ourselves as we move through the world."

She called upon the room for volunteers. The whole room put up their hands. Merenya selected five people in the room to act as examples.

Merenya had everyone stand in a comfortable, easy posture. She took a good look at the first girl standing in line. "See how her one foot is pointing off to the side?"

This girl had her right foot facing the crowd and her left foot pointing to the side of the room. She was leaning heavily on the left.

"She has 'one foot out the door'. Do you feel like that in your endeavours and personal relationships?" Merenya asked the girl. "Do you feel as though you want to go 'all in' but you seek to always have a way out of the situation or a back door you can escape from?"

The girl looked stunned. "Yes! That's a huge part of my personality I've been working to overcome!"

"You can make a conscious effort to stand with both feet pointing forward, then!" Merenya told the girl. "Your subconscious mind is continually thinking of a way to get out of a situation. By pointing your feet—which are connected to your crown chakra— toward your subject, you will naturally begin to feel more invested in it!"

The girl moved her feet so that both were facing forward. Merenya gave her a thumbs up. "I think you'll find an acceleration on that inner work once you start portraying it in the outer world."

After Merenya had assessed the first group, she asked for a second. Nicole and I both put up our hands. Who wouldn't want to be read?

Merenya looked around the room and selected people from the standing rows. She called on both Nicole and I to come up to be read.

I was first in line. Merenya looked at my face before anything else.

"Your forehead is most prominent at the top, meaning you are quite the dreamer and are in touch with the higher realms of thought," she began. "You have a creative mind, but sometimes this can manifest as being somewhat out of touch with reality."

She had me turn so that I faced her with a profile view. She pointed toward my spine. "Do you see this curve? Right behind the solar plexus? Are you standing in your personal power right now or do you feel like you are giving it away?"

I knew as soon as she asked this had to do with Jordan. I wasn't standing in my power. I was giving it away to an ultimatum and to the possibility there was still a future for the two of us. My power was in my spiritual practice and its growth was limited as long as I was still caught in my relationship. "I'm giving it away."

"I could tell. The back of our bodies represents the energy we keep for ourselves, and yours is showing a deficit. You can help to fix this by tilting your pelvis and tucking your tailbone," Merenya instructed. "I have a feeling, though, that you will be through this soon. Your gaze is turned upwards, meaning that you are looking toward the future."

I was comforted by her words. I did my best to tuck my tailbone and neutralize my pelvis so the curve in my back appeared natural.

Merenya moved to Nicole next. "You have a large heart container and I can see you put a lot of care and thought into the relationships you develop by making sure the people you care about are taken care of."

She asked Nicole to turn around so she could make note of a feature on Nicole's back. "See this hollow? Right between the shoulder blades?"

Merenya asked Nicole to face the front again so she could speak with her eye-to-eye. "You give away so much of yourself to others that sometimes you don't give enough back to yourself."

Nicole's eyes widened. Merenya continued, "You'll need a little more self-care so you can show up for yourself first. By taking good care of the Self, you will then have more to offer the people you care about."

I looked at Nicole. Merenya's words could not have spoken more truth. Nicole was my best friend and not once had she ever told me she was too busy to talk when I needed an ear. I could call her at any time of the day and she would have words of encouragement and support to offer me. She was the most caring girl I had ever known.

Nicole wasn't necessarily hard on herself, but she was rather humble. She didn't like to take credit for her kindness. She felt uncomfortable when she was given praise. I agreed with Merenya's statement. Nicole could use a little self-affirmation that she was the absolute best when it came to being present for those she cared about.

Merenya finished reading the other girls in line. Each person affirmed Merenya's statements held truth for them. She caught on to the smallest things, from how a person held their arms to the way they looked at the room. It was incredible.

Nicole and I both walked out of the workshop feeling like we had learned a lot, but also there was so much we didn't know.

"I want inside Merenya's mind," Nicole said as we were en route to our next class. "I want to read people like she does."

"Maybe she'll hold a course sometime!" I said. Merenya had mentioned at the start of class that she had received her training abroad and that seemed like a very far way to go.

At the end of the weekend, the very last workshop was one on assists. It was taught once again by Spencer Hade.

The class was being taught in the most beautiful room I had been in all weekend. It was a large space with windows lining the right side of the entrance. The windows were facing the mountain outside with a little clearing between the distant cliffside and the building.

"Welcome," Spencer said over another microphone. "In this class we will be learning the basic art of Yoga Assists."

Nicole and I had our mats side by side again. We already had the silent understanding we would be partners for the workshop.

"There are three kinds of assists you can provide," Spencer began. "The first is a verbal assist. You can tell someone to draw in their ribcage or straighten a knee. The second is a physical assist—which we will be learning—where you physically adjust the yogi in practice. The third assist is a passive one. By turning your gaze on your subject, often when the adjuster comes around, the yogi fixes themselves!"

The class laughed.

Spencer continued, "We will partner up today and work through a sun and salutation."

She walked us through the lesson. Spencer taught us how to perfect *Samastitihi* and how to support a *Chaturanga*. She demonstrated how to elongate the upward dog and deepen the downward.

I was impressed by her ethics involved in the instruction, how to be hands-on and yet respectful of the bodies handled. How to step in and step out in a way that let the practitioner know when you arrive and depart. The art of assists was like a dance and I loved it.

Spencer played the recording of a sun and salutation vocal track and walked around the room to help us with our assists. Nicole and I laughed together quietly as we adjusted each other. I was perfectly in my element and this was one of my favourite classes of the weekend. I loved it when adjusters came around to offer me assists during a class, and it was fascinating to learn how to do it myself.

After the class closed, Nicole and I noticed a line of yogis waiting to speak with Spencer. We both wanted to say thank you. I felt so strongly that I wanted to give her compliments from my experience. We joined the line for the chance to extend our kind thoughts. Her classes inspired me. From the most challenging class I had ever experienced at the opening ceremony to this assists class, it was clear that Spencer was a talented teacher.

"How was the festival?" Spencer asked with bright eyes when we reached the front of the line.

"So amazing, we loved it!" I replied. "I just wanted to say that of all the classes and workshops this weekend, this and your opening flow were my favourites. Thank you for teaching. Learning from you was wonderful."

"Oh! Thank you! I'm so happy to hear that," she said. "I'm offering a training in September. Consider it?"

As soon as she said it, I heard the words drop into my heart:

The next chapter.

This was it. This was what was waiting for me at the festival.

It wasn't the destination of this grand Journey—I couldn't tell you how I already knew—but a marker along the path I was being called to travel.

A cosmic breadcrumb.

How cute.

The Good Birthday

"Pack a bag, Hallie. We're going on a trip," Jordan told me on the first of June.

"Where to?" I inquired as I looked at the dresser. It was late in the evening and an odd time to be leaving for an excursion.

Jordan just looked at me with a sly grin. "I didn't say 'ask questions' I said 'pack a bag'."

"You gotta give me more!" I exclaimed. "I need to know what to pack for, and for how long! Help me out!"

Jordan rolled his eyes. "Two days. I know you'll want to pack your nice outfits but make sure you have one that's athletic. It will likely be a little warmer than it is here."

My eyes lit up. *Warmer.*

After a frigid winter, I was ready for a getaway.

I leaned over to give Jordan a kiss. "When do we leave?"

"First thing in the morning!" he replied. "So get packing!"

I did as I was told, gathering my favourite early summer outfits and packing them into a duffel. I wondered where we would be going. Jordan didn't mention a specific time so I doubted we would be flying.

Anything east of us would be too far to drive before you finally made it out of the prairies. I surmised that we would either be going south to The States or west toward British Columbia.

I hoped we would be going west.

Jordan left the room as I packed and when I was done, I went out to join him on the couch.

"Why are we going on a trip?" I asked as I sat down beside him to nestle in.

Jordan pulled back and looked at me expectantly.

I stared back at him blankly.

"Hallie... it's your birthday this weekend," he looked somewhat offended.

Oh!

I reeled. My birthday had become something that came and passed unremarkably over the last few years. I hadn't done anything special to celebrate it in a while.

My heart softened. "Oh, Jordan! I wasn't thinking of celebrating."

He kissed the top of my head. "It's okay. I did."

As promised, Jordan set an alarm for early in the morning. He had arranged for one of his friends to come and stay to watch Riggley for the weekend.

I was groggy when I woke up but I helped load the car with our bags and a pack of snacks. I snuck my yoga mat into the back of the trunk also, feeling like I wanted to be prepared for anything. I hopped into the passenger seat once it looked like we were all set.

"You ready?" Jordan asked.

"Ready!" I said, trying to sound chipper despite the remaining morning fog.

The first couple turns confirmed we were not headed for the airport. I was happy with my choice to grab snacks for the road. A significant intersection later and it was clear we were headed westward.

I loved driving through the mountains. Another gift.

Jordan started a podcast as we left the city. He said he already listened to it but thought I would appreciate the episode.

The host talked about the results of a study called the 'Good Friday Experiment'. Apparently they took some people to church and gave half of them magic mushrooms and half of them a stimulant to falsify a 'high'. The host and his guest hilariously went on to talk about what they thought the subjects would experience. Apparently, the psilocybin recipients had 'profound spiritual experiences' during the service.

It seemed like a recipe for an existential crisis to me.

When we passed Banff, I started getting excited. I made the drive to Banff frequently but had not travelled further since the last festival Jordan had gifted me.

As we entered B.C, I was on Social Media looking at tarot decks. Ever since the reading with Nicole, I had become fascinated with the cards. I looked nearly every day, searching for the perfect deck, and recently I came across one I could not get off my mind. The holographic backing caught my attention and the greyscale artistry on their face kept it. They looked sharp against any background and the captions from the creator always hit my heart with feeling. As I navigated myself to the creator's page, my breath hitched and a wave of excitement hit me.

Today, the cards were on sale.

I wanted a tarot deck of my own and these were the cards that I wanted to join me on this adventure I was about to embark on.

I filled in my details and completed the transaction for purchase.

From there on, I was primarily entertained by the scenery. Each tunnel, lake, or wind in the road had me pressed up against the window. I loved travelling through this area because it was so unlike the flat prairies I was used to.

We travelled for most of the day, and in the late afternoon the landscape turned to vineyards and the desert-like hillsides of the Okanagan.

Jordan reached over to put a hand on my thigh. "We're nearly there."

Kelowna! I loved Kelowna.

Jordan adeptly navigated into town. I looked out the window with fascination to see the most magnificent gardens and orchards within the limits of the city.

Eventually we arrived at a house on the side of a golf course, overlooking hillsides and a well manicured green.

"We're here," Jordan told me as he parked the car.

We pulled our bags from the trunk of the car and Jordan went to knock on the door.

I was approaching the front step when the door opened. The lady who answered appeared friendly with white roots showing beneath blonde hair.

"Hello! Welcome to our bed and breakfast!" she greeted us and asked us to come around to the walkout basement which overlooked the hillside. We followed her instructions and discovered a small patio skirted by wild sagebrush and spiky tufts of grass.

The woman met us at the back door and opened it for us. "Make yourselves at home! The bedroom is just to your left."

I put my bags down inside the door as the woman left to return upstairs.

"Check out the mini bar," Jordan nodded toward the corner of the large room we were in.

I took off my shoes and walked over to the area.

Mixologist tools like stirring spoons, a shaker, and a strainer, as well as fancy glasses we could use, were on the counter. I assumed it was a bring-your-own-booze situation as I opened the lower cupboards to find empty shelves.

I raised my eyebrow. "Feel like getting spicy tonight?"

Jordan laughed. "I'm beat. I've got everything planned for tomorrow..."

I walked back to Jordan to help him with the bags, "Thank you for doing the driving today."

He kissed me as he pulled out his toiletries to get ready for bed. "Anytime, babe."

I woke up at dawn the next morning.

Quietly creeping out of bed, I grabbed my yoga mat and laptop, then headed out to the patio while Jordan was still waking for the day.

Setting up my laptop on one of the patio chairs, I found a generic yoga playlist online to quietly accompany me.

Finally, I felt confident in my ability to practice on my own. I set up my phone to record, then stood tall at the top of my mat.

Following my breath, I began to move.

Rise, fall, half lift, fall, jump, lower, stretch, press, hold.

I flowed through three cycles of *Suryanamasakara*, holding *Adho Mukha Savasana* for three breaths each time.

After attending the yoga festival, I dedicated myself to learning the Sanskrit words of the sun salutation. Spencer inspired me to advance my knowledge.

I continued to move through several standing poses, then a few seated ones.

When I was nearing the end of my practice, Jordan came out with two steaming cups of coffee.

"Where did you find those?" I asked.

"The lady upstairs heard your music and came down with them," he said as he sat down at the small table next to the door. "There's breakfast if we want it."

My tummy rumbled.

"Breakfast please!" I said as I rocked through some last motions before rolling up into a seat.

I held my hands out to accept the cup of coffee as Jordan reached over and passed it to me. "It's a nice morning."

I stayed on my mat as I viewed the scene overlooking the patio, sipping the morning brew. I took a deep breath of crisp, fragrant air. "It is."

I looked up and smiled. This had been a very thoughtful and significant gesture on Jordan's part. "Do I get to know what's on the to-do list or no?"

"Nope, today is a day of surprises." He looked stoic, as if keeping our itinerary to himself was a serious affair. "You done? Let's grab something to eat."

I returned my belongings back to our bedroom and followed Jordan up the stairs, arriving in a quaint but inviting kitchen. To our left was a breakfast nook under a window overlooking the course. It had cozy beige and navy plaid bench cushions with navy and dusty yellow accent pillows. There were glasses of orange juice at two place settings I assumed were ours.

The kind lady was at the stove, lifting a lid off a pan of basted eggs. "Sit down, I'm almost done."

She nodded toward the two seats in the nook. I followed Jordan into the second seat and reached for my orange juice to take a sip. It was tangy and sharp on my tongue. I sipped it again to refresh the flavour.

"So what are the two of you here for?" our gracious chef inquired, "I saw your license plate, you're from out of province?"

"It's Hallie's birthday," Jordan confided. "This weekend is her gift."

"Happy birthday!" the woman said as she flipped bacon from the oven onto a plate. "This is a great area to explore! What's on the agenda?"

Jordan looked at me. "She's not allowed to know."

The woman raised an eyebrow.

I smiled. "I trust him. Today is going to be lovely."

"Well, please make sure you catch a winery along your travels. There are so many in the area and you can't go wrong with any of them," our host brought over two plates with bacon, eggs, melon, and strawberries, setting them down in front of us.

I marveled at the breakfast in front of me. "Thank you!"

The woman smiled, "Bon appétit."

"If we were going to a winery, which would you recommend?" Jordan asked.

"The Willow's Wandering is my personal favourite. They have food and drink and will let you wander the vineyards until well after dark," she replied as she began to wash the pan she had cooked our eggs in.

Jordan nodded and took a bite of bacon.

I ate my breakfast quickly, excited for the day ahead. Taking a last drink of my orange juice, I looked over at Jordan who was finishing his breakfast also.

He took my plate to stack on top of his, making it easy to clear the dishes. "Are you going to eat that?"

Jordan was looking at my last unfinished bite of bacon.

"All yours!" I laughed, offering it to him.

Once the dishes were in the sink, we expressed well wishes for the day ahead and retired downstairs to get ready for our adventures.

"You're going to want to wear something easy to move in," Jordan told me as we were getting ready.

I was already wearing comfortable capri leggings from my yoga practice and decided to change from a flowy top to a fitted one. I slipped on my favourite racerback and braided the front sections of my hair until they could fit into a ponytail.

I swiped mascara on and picked my running shoes over my fashionable ones, turning to Jordan once I was ready. He grabbed his wallet and keys. "Good to go?"

I nodded.

I followed Jordan out to the car, feeling buzzing tingles of anticipation. Knowing Jordan's gift for attentiveness, I was sure that whatever we were going to do would be something he knew I would love.

As we drove through the inner-city vegetable patches and orchards, I looked out the window. I loved the vibe here. It was so homely and at the same time somewhat exotic compared to the prairies I was used to.

"Do you ever go somewhere and wonder what it would be like to live there?" I asked Jordan.

"Are you asking me if I want to move here?" He looked over at me, almost concerned.

"No, no. That's not what I'm getting at." I laughed at his expression. "I just mean that our days are influenced by where we live. If we lived somewhere else, it would be a completely different setting for your life. I guess I just imagine putting myself in the shoes of someone who does live here and wonder what that experience would be like."

Jordan shook his head. "Sometimes I wonder what goes on inside your mind."

"What?" I prodded. "You don't think about things like that?"

"Im kidding, Hallie," Jordan replied softly. "I just wonder how you're always coming up with thoughts like that."

Feeling slightly self-conscious at his words, I crossed my arms and continued to look out the window. Jordan was pretty accepting of my existential thought patterns, but I hoped to engage him in a conversation.

The scenery was shifting into a more forested area. We were heading up the side of a mountain. I started to think of the adventure we were about to embark on, deciding it likely to be a hike of some sort.

Jordan turned off the main road and onto a somewhat concealed unpaved back road.

"The reviews said this road was a bit of an ordeal," he said as we hit our first pothole, warning me of the quality of our ride.

We were headed up the side of the mountain on a zig-zagging road where we navigated dips and bumps and I was rocking in my seat. The deeper in we got, the more excited I became.

"Nearly there," Jordan said as we were nearing the top. The trees were starting to thin and I could see a parking lot up ahead.

I leaned over the console between us and kissed Jordan on the shoulder. "Are we here?"

"I believe so," Jordan said as he pulled into a parking spot.

I caught a flash of motion in the rear window. Two couples on bicycles rode past our car. I looked at Jordan suspiciously. "We are at the top of a mountain. Why are there bicycles?"

Jordan grinned. "We're not downhill biking, I promise. I knew you would hate that."

"So we are biking?" I asked, starting to wiggle in my seat.

Jordan nodded as he opened his door. "We are biking."

I got out of the car and stretched. It was going to be a lovely day today. The sun was high with hardly a cloud in the sky. I could feel a slight breeze, but it didn't make me feel chilled. In fact, the whispers of air over my arms felt rather pleasant.

Jordan procured a backpack out of the backseat and tossed a few water bottles inside. "Ready? I think the bike rentals are this way."

I skipped into sync with his steps, reaching for his hand and grasping it with enthusiasm. "What is the trail called?"

"Myra Canyon." Jordan squeezed my hand. "I found it on Social Media, and I knew immediately that you would love it."

We rounded a turn and came across rows upon rows of bicycles. To the left was a little kiosk with a short line of people waiting. We stepped into the queue.

A man with a tablet approached us. "Hi there! I can get you started. This is the line for payment, but I can fill in your waiver and select your bikes while you wait."

He asked us for our height and read a waiver before passing us the tablet to sign.

"I'll have your bikes at station three," he said as both Jordan and I signed the electronic form.

"Thank you," Jordan said as the man walked away. We were at the front of the line and Jordan turned his attention to the kiosk attendant to pay for our rentals.

"Can I pitch in at some point of this vacation?" I asked quietly.

Jordan gave me a piercing look. "Not. A. Chance."

I frowned but didn't push the matter further. Jordan led the way to the sign that said '3' where we found two bikes waiting for us.

After a few minor adjustments to the seat, I found a comfortable height and walked the bike out of the waiting station and onto the main path.

I mounted the bike and waited for Jordan with one foot on the pedal, ready to start the adventure.

I closed my eyes. The trees rustled softly and distant laughter rippled like wind chimes. The sun warmed my skin. I took a deep breath.

This was such a thoughtful gift, and I hadn't even begun the experience.

"Having a moment?" Jordan asked as he pulled up beside me.

I opened my eyes and smiled. "I'm calling in gratitude, and it's all thanks to you."

Jordan looked pleased. "Let's go then! The trail awaits."

I stepped on the pedals and steadied the handlebars as I began to move forward. The path was gravel and there were vibrations radiating through my hands as I began to pick up speed.

The trail started off outlined simply by trees and bushes until it opened up and we could see the valley below. I noted evidence of fire damage as some of the tree trunks were barren and white along the sides of the path.

"This is gorgeous," I yelled over my shoulder to Jordan who was just behind me.

"You haven't even seen the best part yet!" I heard his wind-muffled reply.

I could see ahead of me the path was about to curve through the rock face of the mountain. As we rode into the curve, suddenly the path was outlined by red, towering rock. I stopped pedalling and allowed the bike to coast for a moment as we rode through the pass. The cliff was jagged in places and chiselled in others. Layers of shades and shadows told the past lives of the mountain.

As we continued around the curve, I was entirely preoccupied looking above and beside me. By the time I noticed the tunnel, it was a mere moment before being enveloped in darkness.

Surprised, I let out a squeal. I loved tunnels. Even as a girl they excited me. The absence of light once you've passed its portal and entered into the depths had felt mysterious and novel back then. Truthfully, it still did.

I restrained the urge to let out a loud and glorious "WOOOO" as there were other bikers still passing us.

I looked back at Jordan who was now silhouetted against the light of the entrance. "This is definitely the best part."

I saw him imperceptibly shake his head at me.

There must be something ahead of me. Jordan was expecting to see something that we had not yet come across. I pedalled faster.

I approached the end of the tunnel. The moment the dark walls ceased to surround me, the path opened up to the most beautiful sight.

Trestles.

There were old wooden train trestles connecting the hillsides which were now our biking path.

I could see we were approaching the first one. I slowed the bike to a stop. I wanted to capture this view!

Jordan stopped his bike behind me. "Photo time?"

I smiled at him and took out my phone. "Please."

We climbed to the top of a large boulder that overlooked the path. Jordan took a few of me before I asked for the phone and flipped the camera so that I could take a few selfies of the two of us.

After we were done I leaned into Jordan for a deep kiss.

"This is amazing," I mumbled into his lips.

"Are you happy?" he asked.

"Oh yes, quite!" I laughed as Jordan nodded in approval.

We continued along the trail, taking sporadic photos of the view and stopping for water. With the sun high and our brows speckled in sweat, we reached the largest of the trestles.

I stopped the bike in the middle and pulled off to the side. Jordan did the same and sat on the edge of the trestle, allowing his feet to dangle off the edge. I went to sit next to him.

We hadn't talked about my cosmic request since that night in the park and yet it was suddenly on my mind as I sat next to Jordan.

There was still a significant part of me that wanted this. Jordan had always known how to fulfil my desire for an adventurous life and this was the perfect example of it. Sure, he didn't always buy into my metaphilosophical thoughts, and we were still figuring out how to argue constructively, but he knew how to convince me that I was living my best life with him by my side.

I almost had to shake my head to remember why I was going through this. The promise of something more waiting for me beyond this life.

What if Jordan pulled through? What if all this was him leading up to a declaration that he was ready to do the work to stay? What if my future, my path, was not alone as I envisioned? Would I be working against The Universe?

I shook my head at the thought.

Jordan noticed. He pulled his arm around my shoulders and asked, "What's going on in that head of yours?"

I took a moment to respond. "I'm thinking about the future. When I went to the Yoga Festival I met a teacher I resonated with. I'm thinking about starting my teacher training with her in the fall."

Jordan looked at me suspiciously. "That doesn't seem like something to shake your head at."

I squirmed. I hoped to avoid the topic of conversation that passed through my thoughts, but Jordan was perceptive as always.

"I'm just wondering if I'm doing all the right things..." I said quietly.

Jordan gave me a squeeze. "Hallie, you are one of the most dedicated people I know. You alway try to do the right thing which I admire.

Don't get yourself down about the choices you're making. Keep moving forward and we'll get through this, together."

Together.

I took a deep breath, certain his words meant he was close to being ready to tell me those three little things. I rested my head on his shoulder, deciding to wait for the moment he must have planned. "Thank you, Jordan."

We turned back after sharing a long kiss on the edge of the trestle. As I rode, I allowed myself to dream of the next time we would share such a beautiful moment.

We arrived back at the bed and breakfast near the end of the day. Both Jordan and I freshened up for dinner. I curled my hair and put on the most sophisticated outfit I had brought: a lace top paired with polka dot high-waisted capris.

I knew Jordan was going to make this another special memory as he put on one of his expensive shirts and pulled out all the stops to look nice, including adding a spritz of cologne.

After I had my makeup done and felt ready to go, I turned to Jordan and gave him a long hug, inhaling his scent.

"You look so handsome," I told him.

Jordan took my face in his hands and looked into my eyes. "You are the most beautiful girl I have ever met. I love you, Hallie."

I smiled. "I love you, too."

Jordan released my face and kissed my forehead. "Dinner?"

"Yes!"

Jordan took my hand and kept hold of it as we walked to the car. He opened the door for me like a gentleman and drove us across the lake into wine country.

I didn't ask where we were going. I trusted Jordan to choose the perfect place for tonight.

Jordan adeptly navigated us to a property on the edge of Okanagan Lake. A sign welcomed us at the entrance.

Willow's Wandering.

Of course. This mystical-sounding vineyard was stunning. As we rounded the drive, we were met by a grove of weeping willow trees. My eyebrows lifted with excitement.

The building before us was constructed of windows and wooden features which looked quite sharp in the whispering shadows of the trees. Jordan parked the car and led us through dangling strands of leaves along the path to the winery.

When we arrived, Jordan had a reservation for us.

"When did you make that? I asked as we were seated at a table overlooking the vineyards and the lake.

"This was always the plan. I just confirmed that I picked the best one over breakfast this morning." He smirked as he unrolled his cutlery and placed the napkin on his lap.

I was in awe of his dedication to the details of this trip.

I ordered a refreshing Sauvignon Blanc and Jordan ordered an Old Fashioned. We talked lightly about Jordan's work and my experience at the Yoga Festival with Nicole.

Our dinner arrived as I was telling him how much I loved the assists class and how that had confirmed that I wanted to train under Spencer Hade, elaborating on my earlier comments.

"You should try some of that on me when we get home," Jordan requested as the server put a lamb chop in front of him.

I accepted my well-plated honey butter glazed duck and thanked our server.

"You mean you want to do yoga with me?" I teased.

"Sure, I bet you'll make a great teacher." He smiled at me.

As I separated a bite of my meal with my fork, I ensured that I included the carrot mash and dark cherry puree with a slice of duck. The sweetness of the carrot, earthiness of the cherry, and richness of the duck paired perfectly with the Sauvignon Blanc I sipped to moisten my palate.

After enjoying our meal, Jordan ordered us a glass of Riesling each as our server invited us to walk the vineyards before it got dark.

We held hands through the rows of grape-adorned trellises, embracing the view of the lake.

When we reached the centre of the vines, Jordan turned to me and held out his glass. "Happy birthday, Hallie, I hope you had an amazing day. Cheers!"

I laughed and touched my glass to his.

The moment our glasses made contact, my eyes widened with recognition.

Two glasses of wine clinking in a vineyard.

Jordan noticed a palpable shift in my demeanor after our walk at Willows Wandering. I was lost in thought, my mind racing through the other visions of my Journey. He didn't say anything directly, but I could tell he was regarding me more cautiously, as he normally did when I went quiet.

We were nearly silent on the drive back. I kept my gaze out the window wondering about my future, my path, my... calling. Jordan didn't ask any intrusive questions to uncover my inner thoughts.

After we arrived back at the bed and breakfast, our host recommended taking a walk to a viewpoint overlooking the whole valley and city of Kelowna. Jordan and I walked up a short trail in the neighbourhood to arrive at the top of a hill.

The sprawling lights of the city were beautiful, with twinkles of headlights highlighting the roadways below and clusters of porch lights illuminating the homes of the wealthy on the higher ridges.

The moon was not yet full but bright enough to light our surroundings in a soft blue-white glow as we sat on a large boulder. Jordan brought a bottle of sparkling, a pair of glasses, and a second smaller bag. He poured drinks for us in celebration and kissed me sweetly.

"Did you have a good birthday?" he asked as he pulled away.

I smiled, looking down at my hands. My mind quickly replayed all the memories I could file from the wonderful day we had shared together.

"It was amazing, Jordan, of course I did. Thank you so much for making this happen." I put my head on his shoulder.

We looked out onto the vista in front of us. A slight breeze caused us to draw closer to each other.

"I have something else for you," Jordan said as he pulled over the second bag. "It's not much but I thought I'd give you something, too."

"Oh, Jordan! This trip would have been enough!" I said.

"I know," he replied. "I just wrote you something special."

This was it. As he placed the second bag in front of me I reached for the card inside and held it in my hands for a moment. I was excited to read these words which must surely be the ones I had been asking him to say. Here, after a beautiful day and contained inside a beautiful moment I knew that I was soft, open, ready to receive, and ready to shift.

I opened the card and read beautiful words. A love note. A pouring of his heart. Another confirmation of how much he adored me.

But no words about himself.

No confirmation that he also adored himself.

I deflated internally but kept my chin high so I didn't give myself away. I looked at him, thanked him, kissed him, and told him it touched my heart. I pulled a candle out of the bag. Sandalwood and Myrr.

"I didn't feel like you should go empty handed on your birthday," he said as he looked at the candle.

He couldn't say it now even with all of this work to keep me. He knew that there was a chance I would walk away and I had given him the key that would anchor me to stay. Yet here on this hill, in this intimate moment, the gift that would have granted him what he sought from me wasn't present. If he had really been ready to embrace our future, he would have honoured my request. Now would have been 'the' moment.

"You've been so sweet this weekend and I really appreciate it. I'll keep all of this close to my heart," I said. I meant it, now acutely aware that this could be one of our last grand moments to cherish together. "I love you."

We stayed on the top of the hill for a while longer, finishing our sparkling wine as we enjoyed the sight and the company of each other before returning to the bed and breakfast.

I think Jordan believed that if he showed me that he could rise to give me everything that I loved that it would be enough to convince me to keep him. That's not what I needed to anchor me, though.

I needed to hear those three little things.

Eight of Swords

ONCE JORDAN AND I returned to the city, Jordan returned to work and I was left to contemplate what had been missed over the weekend.

Our lease expired on Friday. Jordan would be back Thursday evening. We were quite literally at the final crossroads, and I was preparing myself for the goodbye I knew was quickly approaching.

Wednesday afternoon, I sat with my pen hovering over a piece of paper for an hour. Two crumpled attempts sat beside me and the perfect words my heart wanted to share escaped me. I hoped to write Jordan a letter so that I could say what I needed without getting emotional. I didn't trust myself not to.

My phone chirped on the counter behind me.

> Happiest of Birthdays! I hope you had an amazing day!

It was Maxille.

> Thank you! It was a lovely weekend.

I looked at the most recent attempt at writing my letter. The few words that I had written sounded ingenuine and forced. I sighed and started to crush the page in my palms.

> Are you free today by any chance? I could use some help settling into my new place.

I wrote back quickly, seizing the chance to distract myself.

> Sure! Send me the address and I'll come over!

I missed the opportunity to help Maxille move over the weekend but the least I could do was help her organize and arrange her new space.

Not wanting to leave my discarded letters out while I was away, I picked up the papers and gathered the trash bag to dispose of them together. I placed the bag at the door as I walked to the bathroom to check my appearance.

I decided that a spritz of dry shampoo and a few swipes of mascara would make for a passable look before moving to the bedroom to change out of my home clothes.

As I reached the dresser, Jordan's card from our last night in Kelowna was on the top of it still. I hadn't had the heart to put it away yet. I lifted the card up to read the words again and felt a flush of sadness rise to my cheekbones.

Why?

The familiar question came to the forefront of my mind as my eyes welled with tears. Why hadn't he honoured my cosmic request on that hill? Was he still planning on pulling through for us? If he couldn't, this would crush him. Why couldn't he see that?

It was the hurt, the pain, the loss that I wanted to sidestep, but without Jordan rising to my request, it would be unavoidable. It wouldn't matter how thoughtfully I composed a letter, his heart would break at my words.

I hadn't expected Jordan to leave it to the last moment either. It held less significance for him to say it now, at the final hour.

I thought of his tardiness like a late arrival at my metaphorical graduation ceremony. Where the ushers were now using flashlights, the Master of Ceremonies was arriving on stage and I was watching the seat he was supposed to take sit empty.

There are certain times in life where punctuality makes all the difference in how one views their importance in your world.

My phone chimed again.

Max had shared her location.

I wiped my eyes, thankful the tears hadn't spilled over and pulled on a pair of jeans. Riggley hardly lifted his head as I got my things together. His eyebrows raised in my direction but was otherwise settled on the bed.

Once ready, I grabbed the trash and took it out on my way to the car.

The first thing I noticed about the house in front of me was the planter boxes out front with dead, yellow growth from last year, a project I was sure Max would be keen to tackle.

Here

I sent her a message as I walked up the path to the house, giving her some notice before I knocked. It looked like an older home and the lower windows were so grimy I couldn't tell if there was a curtain shading them or not.

I could hear footsteps at the door as I arrived.

"Hello, my dear!" Maxille opened the door with a grin on her face. "Welcome to my new abode!"

The house was a bilevel split, and a set of stairs welcomed me as I entered. A stale, musty scent also greeted my arrival but I ignored it as I gave Max a big hug and asked where we could start.

"Down here!" She took my hand. "Keep your shoes on."

I wondered why I needed shoes but quickly understood as I allowed Max to lead me to her room.

We descended the stairs which were lined in an outdated shiplap material and landed on the lower level. The carpet crunched slightly as I made contact and I let out an audible sound of surprise and stifled disgust.

"There was a small flood right before I moved in and they haven't replaced the carpet yet," Max explained.

"Was your room affected?" I asked.

"Just the entry, but not the whole room," she said as we turned right and entered her bedroom.

The yellow shag carpet with a discoloured circle at the door made the first impression. Maxille's takeover made the second.

Boxes and belongings were piled in one corner of the room and on a nesting couch in the other.

"When is the carpet getting replaced?" I asked.

"Over the weekend, hopefully." Max replied. "Which, I was hoping you might be available to join me on a retreat I was invited to…"

"Oh?" I would do anything for a getaway this weekend. Any reason to escape the outcome of my ultimatum would be appreciated. "What's the retreat?"

"It's a Summer Solstice Gathering just outside town," Max explained. "One of the owners of a studio in town has land in the foothills and he opens up the property for people to camp. There's workshops and classes for our little yoga community."

"I'd love to come! That sounds incredible!" I was excited to leave for the weekend and escape the catastrophe of my impending breakup.

"Yay!" Max cheered. "I have all the camping equipment so you just need to bring yourself and your yoga mat, and maybe some warm clothes for the evenings."

"That's perfect!" I laughed as I went to sit on the bed.

"Oh! Don't sit there." Max tried to catch me.

My weight was already falling and as I hit the mattress, a crunching sound precipitated the bed jerking and suddenly dropping a few inches.

I couldn't help but laugh as I stood back up. "Oh Max, is your bed broken?"

She nodded. "I've been promised it will be replaced with the carpet, but for now I don't want my bed right on the floor."

I was shocked at the living conditions she had moved into, but I didn't want to come across as critical or pessimistic.

"Well hopefully this weekend will provide new circumstances for your bedroom," I said, hoping she heard the positivity I was trying to convey. "What can I help you with?"

"Can I be honest with you, Hallie?" Max looked at me intently.

"Of course!"

"I think I'm being way too positive about this space. It was affordable, and it was closer to the inner city, but I'm not sure I can stay here."

I didn't blame her one bit, and in that moment I could see a possible way out. "Can you hold on for one more week?"

Max's expression changed to one of curiosity.

"Jordan's at his last chance. He has until Friday to complete a task I set for him, or else I am going to be signing our lease by myself. If that happens, I could use a new roommate and uh... you can go barefoot in my suite if you like."

"Oh, Hallie, we would be the best of roommates," she said. "What if Jordan stays, though?"

My heart twinged. At this point my faith in him pulling through was holding by worn thread. The card on the dresser said everything and nothing. Still, I intended to give him until Friday as promised.

"Then I will personally help you find a new place," I offered. "Let's see what the weekend brings us both, and then we can make some decisions."

"I guess I don't need to unpack everything today in that case..." Max looked around at her belongings.

I stood quietly beside her as she decided what to do.

"Well, this was more helpful than I anticipated. Thank you, sweet thing." She reached for my hand and squeezed it.

"Do you still need my organizational services?" I asked.

"No, it doesn't appear that I do. I'll just wait this out and see what happens, but I really appreciate that you're willing to offer your spare room." Max sounded genuine.

"Of course! So... this weekend. Let's plan the details!"

When I got home, the girls were playing in the backyard.

"Hallie!" they yelled as I opened the gate from the parking pad. Dropping their bubble wands, they came to greet me.

"Hello, Fable. Hi, Brook!" I knelt down to give them hugs.

"Hi! Mom said you do yoga," Fable stated directly.

Surprised, I answered, "Yes, I do!"

"We wanted you to come camping with us. Mom said you were doing yoga," her words explaining the comment.

Danielle must have seen my posts on Social Media.

"I was doing yoga, she's right. Did you have fun camping?" I asked.

Fable proceeded to regale me of her new friends and the activities they participated in as I picked up one of the bubble wands and blew large orbs for Brook to catch.

Brook loved chasing the bubbles and making them pop. She would prance around with her eyes darting between the bubbles, deciding which one to target.

After a few minutes of this I asked the girls, "Do you want to help me teach Riggley a new trick?"

"Can he roll over?" Brook asked.

"He sure can!" I had taught him several months ago. 'Crawl' was proving more challenging. "Let's put the bubbles away!"

Fable helped gather the wands and secured them into their soapy cylinders. She gave them to me as we walked to my doorstep and I placed them at the gate.

I opened the door to find Rigs patiently waiting at the base of the stairs, sitting.

"Okay girls, shoes off up here." I removed my footwear and descended two steps to give them room.

Riggley's tail was swishing in overtime against the tile but he remained at the base of the steps.

When the girls were ready I led them down into my suite.

The tiles were cold as always when my steps reached the bottom. Riggley stood to greet the girls with gentle face-licks, and they returned his welcome by rubbing his ears and patting down his back as he followed me into the kitchen.

"The treats are in the jar on the counter, Fable. Will you grab them when I say so?" I asked.

Fable looked on the side counter and found the jar.

"Down, Stay," I commanded Riggley, who lay down.

I backed away from him as he remained in place at the threshold between hall and kitchen.

"Fable, the treats please," I requested, maintaining eye contact with Riggley, encouraging him to stay in place.

Fable brought the whole jar to my side as Brook followed.

"Tell him [O–K]," I mouthed the word and formed the letters with my right hand in sign-language.

Fable exclaimed, "Okay!"

Riggley came running to us to collect his reward.

"Give him a treat," I told her.

She did.

"Let's teach him how to crawl," I told the girls.

"Down," I told Rigs. "Stay."

"Brook, can you put out five treats in a line?" I asked, knowing she would love this task.

Brook evenly spaced out the morsels from us halfway to the wall at the edge of the cabinets.

I went to the fridge and retrieved a slice of deli meat, tearing off a small piece and handing it to Fable who had moved to the end of the treats. Then, straddling over Riggley, I commanded, "Crawl."

Rigs, knowing that any word in that tone was meant for him, started to get up and move toward the line of treats. With my hands, I pushed on his hips to keep them low to the floor.

The girls squealed every time he reached and licked up a treat. By the third treat, I relaxed pressure on his hips. He continued to move toward the final treat with his hips down.

"Yes! Crawl," I affirmed. "Fable, go ahead."

Fable gave Riggley his earned reward as he got up and snarfed it out of her hands. Fable and Brook's giggles sounded at Rig's enthusiasm.

"Let's do it again," I suggested, having Rigs turn around by leading a treat under his nose until he was facing the other way.

"Down, Stay," I commanded as I dropped the treat.

Rigs complied as he chewed.

"Brook, only three treats this time. Same distance, please." My voice softened when speaking to the girls.

Three treats were placed at even distance and the girls took their spot at the end. I ripped off another piece of the deli meat and handed it to Fable again.

"Crawl," I said firmly as I gently hovered over Riggley's hips.

This time, Riggley needed only the gentle reminder of my hands but otherwise moved forward with his hips down.

When he reached the last treat I was so proud. "Yes! Good boy!"

"Good boy, Riggley!" Brook cheered him on.

Fable delivered the deli meat.

"One more time! I think he's almost got it," I told the girls.

Leading Rigs to turn around with another treat, this time I placed him in front of me and scootched back so there was space between us. The girls came to stand behind my shoulder.

Riggley automatically went into a down position, having figured out a routine to our session.

I looked him in the eyes and made the hand signal I wanted to associate with the trick. As I drew my finger in a straight line in the air, I told him, "Crawl."

I put the treat down just in front of my knees, hiding it with my hand.

Riggley looked down at the treat and for a moment looked as if he would get up to retrieve it.

His front paws took two little shuffles.

Riggley's hips began to lift as he pressed forward, but quickly returned to the ground.

He crawled.

When he reached my hand, I revealed the treat and let him have it.

"Yes! Who is such a good boy?" I gave him rough scruffs behind the ears as the girls cheered behind me.

"Fable! Deli meat!" I requested.

Fable went to the counter where I had left the slice of deli and ripped off a larger piece of his reward, laughing as Rigs ate it out of her hands.

"Brook! Do you want to try?" I asked, wanting to include both girls.

With all the excitement, Riggley was circling the girls.

I got up and led Rigs so there was space between him and Brook.

Making the non-verbal commands, I asked him to settle into position.

Riggley lay down and waited.

"Brook, do you remember what hand signal I used?" I asked.

She nodded.

"Then go ahead," I offered.

Brook, taking her job seriously looked to Riggley. He stayed, waiting for a command.

"Crawl," Brook said in her high voice as she made a line in the air with her little pointer finger. Brook had no treat, and I wondered if Rigs would be motivated enough.

Riggley took just a moment to think about his next actions.

Again, his two front paws shuffled forward.

His hips stayed low.

He crawled on command.

When he reached Brook, Fable was ready with the last of the deli meat, already offering it to him as both girls cheered.

He crawled...

I looked upon my pup, the girls, and my little home. This trick had become the most challenging I taught Riggley, and with a sudden realization I understood it would be the last one he ever learned from me.

"Riggley!" I called him.

He came to me, giving my face a gentle swipe with his tongue. I gave him pets on the top of his head and sunk my hands in the fur of his neck.

Leaning into me, Riggley accepted my pets. I leaned back into him, feeling into the moment and inhaling his scent.

He challenged me to be a better dog-mom and also provided a constant sense of calm. I appreciated him for both.

Standing up, I moved to the girls side, taking the treat jar from Fable.

"Would you like to see his other tricks?" I asked.

"Yes!" the girls said in tandem, making little jumps on the spot. I took a handful of treats from the jar and looked at Riggley.

"Do Yoga," I said in the tone I used for verbal commands.

Riggley stretched his front paws forward and arched his back in the pose 'downward dog' was named after.

"Yes!" I tossed him one of the treats in my hand.

"Now, Spin," I said, moving my hand in a clockwise circle.

Riggley spun on the spot, receiving a reward when he was done.
I made a fist.
Riggley sat.
I put my hand out, at his chest. "Shake."
Riggley put his paw in my hand.
I gave him a treat as I lowered my palm to the ground.
Riggley lay down.
"Are you shy?" I commanded.
Riggley put his paw over his snout and looked away from me.
Another reward.
"Play dead."
A half roll onto his back.
"Roll over."
A full roll, two treats.
"Crawl."
Riggley crawled.

Tears had already formed in my eyes, but the first one broke at the final trick. With the salty trail making its way down my face, I knelt down to love on my good boy.

Fable and Brook cheered, and laughed, and spun around the room.

"That was awesome!"

"Wow!"

"Can he do more?"

I shook my head as I looked up from the pets I was showering Riggley with. "No, that's all I've taught him."

"Are you crying?" Fable stopped to look at me.

Brook stopped, too, her eyes on my face.

"Yes, I am," I said, choosing not to lie. "Teaching him all of these has taken a lot of time."

Both the girls came to hug me and I embraced them as Riggley got up and circled us, sniffing faces.

My phone began to vibrate and ring in my pocket.

As I pulled it out, I saw Jordan's name and photo on the screen.

I answered quickly as the girls pulled away to play with Riggley.

"Hey, Love," I spoke into the phone.

"Hey, do you have a second?" Jordan's voice replied.

"I'm just with the girls, can I take them upstairs and call you back?" I asked.

"Sure, we'll talk in a little bit." Jordan hung up.

I walked over to the girls on the carpet and watched as they threw around a toy duck, Riggley chasing it between them. Their joy and his was infinitely satisfying to watch.

"Girls, it's time to go back upstairs," I called.

Fable dropped the duck back in Riggley's toy bin to the right of the TV as Brook came to hug my legs.

I put a hand on her hair. "Come on, Hunnie."

We started walking to the stairs as Rigs followed behind us.

When we got to the base, I walked the girls up the stairs. We put our shoes on. We walked out the door.

The bubble wands were still by the gate, and I picked them up, bringing them with us upstairs. I opened the gate, and the girls led the way, hopping up their front steps and into their home.

Following behind them, I placed the bubble wands on the ledge.

"I can't stay," I announced to Dani, who was coming around the corner from the living room.

"That's okay, thanks for bringing them back," she said. "I heard them downstairs."

"Yes, we taught Rigs a new trick! They were so helpful," I replied as I heard squeals coming from the bedrooms. A new game must be under way already.

"Alright, well, I won't keep you. Goodnight!" Dani waved as she turned back toward the living room.

I gave a single wave as I retreated back through their doorway.

On the way back to my suite I noticed a parcel preventing the lid of the mailbox from closing at the far edge of the fence. I reached over to grab it. Jordan or I had mail.

I collected the package along with the rest of the accumulated mail and flyers and carried on through the gate.

When I got to the front step I pulled out my phone and called Jordan, taking a seat on the stair and letting the mail sit in my lap.

"Hey," he answered in the first few rings.

"Hey, Love. What's up?"

"I just wanted to see what you were up to this weekend?" Jordan asked.

"Maxille invited me to a retreat this weekend! We'll be leaving early Friday," I told him as I watched a bird land between myself and the gate, pecking at the gravel and weeds lining the walkway.

"Alright, if you'll be away, I'll get out of the house, too. My mom wants me to travel home for the weekend," he told me.

"Okay, that will work." I said, feeling relieved that he wouldn't be alone in the house all weekend. "Any reason why?"

"Pretty sure she's just missing her son," Jordan joked. "This is the longest I've been away, so I figured I should go."

The bird flew up to the top of the fence, preening its wings. "Then go see your momma. I'm sure she'll appreciate it."

"Thanks, Hallie. I'll see you tomorrow when I get home." He started to close the conversation.

"Okay see you tomorrow. I love you." I shifted the mail to pick it up as the bird flew away.

"Love you, too, bye." The call ended.

I sighed and took the mail into the house.

Riggley was waiting at the bottom step, getting up from the floor as I opened the door.

"You are such a good boy, Riggley," I praised him as I took off my shoes and made my way down the steps.

We walked together into the dining room where I deposited the mail on the table, assessing the contents.

I went through the envelopes first, determining most of them to be bills and promotion except the bright yellow one, a card addressed to me with my grandmother's return address. I smiled. It was a birthday card which likely arrived on time but was neglected until today.

Turning my attention to the package, I noticed it was addressed to me as well. Curiously, I sought a steak knife to get through the tape encircling it. I fought with the packaging to reveal what I had purchased.

Once I had the wings of the box open, a layer of crumpled paper was lifted up to reveal a smaller box wrapped in clear plastic.

My tarot deck.

Excitedly, I left the mail at the table and brought my new deck to the couch. I went to the spare room and collected a candle, my quartz, my cedar, and my journal, then brought them back to the living room and placed them on the coffee table.

I carefully unwrapped the deck from its packaging and held the box in my hands for a moment before looking at the cards. Holding them to my chest, I felt a magnetism toward them. A pull, drawing me into the deck.

Lighting the candle, then slowly sliding the cards out of the box, I started by cleansing my deck with cedar smoke. I also knocked them with the knuckles of my closed fist to dispel any energy from their transit through the mail.

I was interested in my new tool and curious to see if it would help. I decided to shuffle the cards and ask for guidance on how to proceed with my unimaginably difficult task ahead. Tomorrow was Jordan's last day to fulfill my cosmic request.

Show me Friday.

As I was about to finish my shuffle and cut the deck, a card jumped out and landed with the holographic backing facing up. I heard 'jumpers' often held special significance in the reading. I left the wayward card aside as I pulled four tarot cards in the same spread I had done with Nicole. Situation. Obstacle. Action. Outcome.

As I flipped them, my first reaction was a response to the beauty of the faces of the cards. All in grayscale, they looked as if they had been sketched with pencil. The first card was a heart, pierced with three swords. The rest of the spread was reversed. A single cup, overflowing. A girl, hands chest level, grasping the hilt of a sword pointed down. Six daggers facing me, all collected in a single hand with one dagger, separate, facing away.

At first glance I became uneasy. As I read through the guidebook, a rock dropped in my chest.

The Situation: THREE OF SWORDS
Heartbreak, bottled thoughts.
Cruel words exchanged between loved ones.

The Obstacle: ACE OF CUPS [REVERSED]
Blocked connection.
Emotional energy is being wasted or lost.

The Action: JUSTICE [REVERSED]
An unjust outcome.
Stop the delay, you need to move forward.

The Outcome: SEVEN OF WANDS [REVERSED]
Destroyed confidence.
Persist in your goal despite opposition.

What a mess, I thought.

After reading the cards and copying the reading into my journal, I turned my attention to the card which had jumped out of the deck.

I flipped it over, and my breath caught in my throat.

A Butterfly. Upside down, surrounded by two swords on each side. Trapped, and beautiful.

EIGHT OF SWORDS [REVERSED]
Release.
You have found the way out. You are free.

I began to cry. It was the same card I had connected with so strongly in Nicole's reading. Instead of a girl surrounded by swords, this card depicted a butterfly. A feeling of peace washed over me as I remembered the message of her reading. The Sun. Everything is going to be okay. I brought the card to my chest and held it against my heart.

Thank you, I offered. *Thank you.*

Ribs vs. Ribcages

Thursday passed without the words I needed from Jordan. He came home in the early afternoon and acted like it was any other day while I waited for an acknowledgment of the occasion. I still had not yet composed my letter, and with Jordan home for the day, there was hardly an opportunity to write one.

My stress was increasing with every hour that passed. An anger settled around the periphery of this anxiety. What was he thinking? Was he oblivious? Had he forgotten? Did he think this did not matter to me? Was he unaware of the stakes?

Just like the Three of Swords had indicated, my frustrations were beginning to simmer. I eventually gave Jordan a kiss goodnight and headed to bed early.

"Goodnight, babe," he returned my kiss briefly before his eyes darted back to the video game he was playing.

Riggley followed me to bed.

I pulled him up to me. He was never a snuggler but I needed his warm body against mine.

He was Jordan's dog and had been with him since puppyhood two years before my arrival.

I buried my face into his scruff, kissing his earthy smelling fur.

We stayed like that for not more than a minute before he wriggled his way out of my embrace and took up his usual spot at my feet.

I looked at Riggley, feeling an aching void in my heart I knew would be his after today.

I stared at the ceiling fiercely. I was not tired. I simply no longer wanted to be in Jordan's presence, pretending everything was alright when that was hardly the case. This was my last night before I was thrown into the unknown.

I should have started my Journey months ago. I should have bravely stepped forward onto my path instead of traipsing this line of fearing to leave Jordan behind.

I had given him the invitation, though. He had just declined to RSVP.

You, alone.

The message had been clear, and The Universe had conspired to make it so.

I needed to honour my cosmic request. Tomorrow, I would leave for the Summer Solstice. Alone.

When I awoke the next morning, I had the butterfly in mind. The reading of yesterday was present in my thoughts, but I could not tell you why I didn't just sit Jordan down after I getting out of bed to give him the hard news as the Justice card had suggested. In the business of packing for the gathering, I also didn't create the opportunity.

I moved about the bedroom, laying clothes out to take with me. Once I was happy with my selections, I walked to the kitchen to eat something for breakfast.

When I saw the state of the counters, I froze as a rush of anger overcame me.

Jordan had decided to slow-roast ribs late in the night before coming to bed, apparently. The kitchen remained a mess of dirty pans and meat still in the slow cooker.

Disgusting.

I ceased my pursuit of breakfast and returned to the bedroom. I packed, moving the clothing I had set out on the bed to inside my duffel bag. As I was getting ready to go, Jordan was moving around me, collecting his things also so that he could leave when I did.

I was fuming as I gathered miscellaneous camping equipment, took a last opportunity to shower, packed my toiletries.

He was going to leave the mess for me to clean.

As I was just about ready to go, Jordan came into the bedroom to kiss me goodbye. His car was already packed, with Rigs in the back seat. His last bag was hitched over his shoulder. He could feel my stiff tension. I allowed him to kiss my cheek but my frustration did not offer a kiss in return.

"What?" he asked.

"Nothing. Have a good weekend." I said, sensing that my tension would be working against me.

"What, Hallie? You won't say goodbye?" he asked again.

"Goodbye, have a good weekend." I gave him a kiss, attempting to soften.

"No, what's wrong?" he pushed. I didn't pause. I didn't take a breath.

"You left all the dishes for me, Jordan." I said.

"And you're mad?" he replied, oblivious.

"Of course I'm mad." My voice began to rise in my frustration. "I'm trying to leave too, and now I have to deal with the mess you've left for me in the kitchen before I can go! What did you think would happen to them? Either I clean it up or it gets left like that for the whole weekend while we're gone. So really, you've made it my job. But go! Have a good weekend."

"What the hell, Hallie?" he defended as he walked out and moved into the kitchen. "Why would you just strut around silently raging at me? If you wanted it done you could have just told me. Not like I have places to be too."

"Seriously? This is your mess!" I snapped back.

"What do you want from me Hallie?" he demanded as he put a pan in the sink.

"Nothing," I replied, angry and desperately wanting the argument to end.

"No, Hallie. What do you want?"

"Nothing!"

"Hallie. What. Do. You. Want. From. Me."

So many thoughts of frustration raced through my mind. I didn't want to be fighting. I never did. I didn't want to get so mad at him. I never did. I didn't want to be the person I am with him.

"I'm done, Jordan!" My voice broke through falling tears.
"Done with WHAT, Hallie!" he yelled, stopping to look at me.
"I'm done with YOU!" I cried, horrified at the words escaping my lips.

There was a moment of silence before Jordan slammed the top drawer of the dishwasher back into place and began to roar. I can't recall the words. I can only recall the reddened face of anger as the hurt hit his heart. The tears in his eyes. The tightness around my chest as he turned on me and walked out the door.
What had I done?
I sat at the edge of the couch with my hands in my palms. The tears falling freely. Breath heaving in my chest.
There was no going back now.

Summer Solstice

I BRUSHED MYSELF OFF from the upset so that I could finish cleaning the kitchen and pick up Maxille for our trip.

I'd experienced the post-breakup phase of shock before, where you're able to function like normal until the reality truly settles in. I think part of me was relieved I was finally on the other side of the knife's edge of my ultimatum. The weight in my chest I had felt for several days was gone. Jordan had not given me what I needed. I would not go back.

"Hey, girl!" Max greeted me as I arrived at her place.

"Hey!" I called from the hatch of my car as I paused to embrace her in a hug.

"My car or yours?" she asked.

"It doesn't matter to me," I replied, "Did you want to drive or be passenger princess?"

"Driver, I think! You can princess for this one!"

We shifted my bags into the back of her car, and I accepted the trip's fruit and veggie offering on my lap before we started to drive away. "How was your week?"

She gave me a pointed look before unraveling. "They're not going to be doing the carpets this weekend, despite me moving all my things into the living room. I hope none of my roommates get curious and go through my things."

I cringed. "Awe, Max, do we have time to go back and move them again?"

"Don't worry about it. It was a pain to move things in the first place and I don't want to do it again," she said before looking at me cautiously. "How did things go this week?"

I hung my head. "I exploded."

"Are you okay?"

Surprisingly I wasn't sad. I was more disappointed in how I chose to conduct myself. "I will be okay. It's over, though."

"Do you still need a roommate then?" she asked as she looked out the front window.

"Unless you'd like to stay where you are?"

"No, thank you!"

The countryside and rolling hills on our way to the gathering were serene. It was a bright and sunny day, with only a few scattered clouds.

Max and I talked about the gathering for the remainder of our trip. She had seen the class schedule and was attempting to relay it to me.

"There's an opening meditation later tonight. Oh! And I'm looking forward to the Kundalini in the loft!" She told me as she kept her eyes on the road.

"The loft?" I asked.

"Yes! I guess most of the classes are held in the loft of the barn," she elaborated.

"A barn." I repeated. "Have you been before?"

"No, I've just heard little bits," she confided. "We're coming up on the town, what do the directions say when we get there?"

I looked down at the set of very detailed directions Max had printed from an email, finding my place.

"Turn right at the stop sign," I told her.

"Just the stop sign?" she asked.

"I'm assuming its the first one we come across on this road," I told her.

She nodded, and after we got a little ways into the town, a stop sign appeared.

"Right?" she asked.

"Right."

She completed the turn and asked, "What's next?"

"Keep on this road for another thirty kilometers," I told her. "Then we have to look for signs when the road forks."

It was the prettiest thirty kilometers I had travelled in this area. The foothills made our road wind between them. Some of the hills held pastures with goats on them. Others had tall trees leading from a gate on the road, around a hill out of sight, indicating a property likely lie beyond. The sun shone on the hillsides, making the green prairie grasses appear bright and vibrant.

Eventually, the pavement did fork into two gravel roads.

"Summer Solstice this way!" Maxille read the sign on the left with the arrow pointing down the road.

The gravel road didn't take long to simply turn into wheel tracks.

"Hey, if you don't want to bottom out your car, drive with one tire on the raised centre and the other off to the side instead of driving in the grooves," I told Max.

She nodded and adjusted her driving to match my suggestion.

We went down a hill, into a small valley with empty pastures on both sides of our little 'road'.

After turning a gentle corner, a barn appeared in the near distance. A large canvas tent was just behind it, sitting in a sizable meadow. People were scattered and mingling amidst the property.

As we approached the barn, a man with fluffy brown hair and an aged, sun-worn face began to approach our vehicle.

Maxille braked enough to come to a slow roll and unrolled her window.

"Hello girls, glad you made it here," he welcomed us.

"Hi there, the instructions were on point!" Maxille laughed as she came to a stop.

"Oh good! We wanted everyone to make it," the man replied. "I'm Maverick. Welcome to my property. There are three places to camp. In the meadow, up the hill, and by the river. Which would you like?"

Maxille and I looked at each other, and as if by telepathy both answered, "the river?"

Smiling, more confidently Maxille told Maverick, "The river, please."

"The river it is," Maverick said as he leaned against the frame of the car. "Go up the lane to the house. You can park at the house as you unpack your vehicle. Go down the path to the right of the house and follow it past the steam hut until you reach the river clearing. When you've unpacked, park the car where the rest are parked before you get to the barn."

Max and I nodded, deciding the directions would make sense as we followed them.

"Thank you," I called across Maxille.

"Thank you," Maxille chimed in.

Maverick nodded and patted the top of the hood twice. "On you go then."

Maxille and I carried on, passing the 'parking lot' of vehicles before the barn, then continuing up the tree-lined lane we reached the house, parking behind a white SUV.

"Hallie!" I heard as we pulled up and got out of the car.

A girl I had always held a genuine adoration toward but had yet to invest time with was coming around the side of the SUV in front of us.

"Amber!" I smiled, greeting her with a hug.

"Max said she was bringing a friend named Hallie, but I didn't put it together that it was you! I'm so happy that it is!" She smiled back at me.

Amber and I had lived parallel to each other, living in the same city, attending the same high school, going to many of the same music festivals, and only crossing paths a handful of times.

I looked at Max. "I didn't know you two talked!"

"Amber was the one who invited me after I went to a class she taught!" Max replied, making sense of the story and giving Amber a hug also.

"Are we camping together then?" I asked, and somewhat suggested.

"Sure are!" Amber smiled. "Follow me! I think I've found the spot."

We gathered as much of the camping gear as we could carry from the back of the car and walked behind the house to find a path to a small cabin.

"This way," Amber called. The path continued behind the cabin and through the trees, turning into a downhill trail of small rocks acting as stepping stones and stairs. It smelled earthy here, like damp grass and tree bark. I could hear the faint sound of rippling water.

Beyond the stepping stones was a grassy pathway I could only assume was still a part of our journey.

"It's just up the pathway," Amber announced as she hoisted a bag to better fit on her shoulder.

We kept walking until we reached the promised clearing. It was right on the edge of the river. Small streaks of blue could be seen through the trees. Dandelions scattered sporadically throughout the tall grass and other weeds. There was already one tent set up.

"I'll help you pitch yours and then we can wander down to dinner," Amber suggested.

Maxille and I got the tent out of the bag and the three of us struggled a little with the tent poles, laughing at times when things didn't work properly but eventually managing to get the tent upright.

I took a second trip to get our sleeping bags and my duffel from the car.

Amber emerged from her own tent just as I arrived into the clearing.

"I'm going to start heading up for dinner. I'll meet you at the kitchen tent?" she said as she zipped up her tent fly.

"Sure, I'll see you there," I answered as I unzipped my own.

"Hi!" I greeted Max as I entered the tent.

She was stringing fairy lights to the inner ties. "We should be able to see our tent if we get back after sunset now."

"What a smart thought!" I complimented.

We rolled out our bedding and got everything prepared so that when we got back, the tent would be ready for bedtime.

"Dinner?" Max asked when all was set.

"Yes, lets head out." I collected the dishware we were asked to bring with us and left the tent.

As we headed back up the path to the car, we found Amber again just outside the cabin.

"What is this?" I asked, nodding toward the cabin door.

"It's the steam hut!" she said excitedly.

Mavericks directions suddenly clicked.

Two people walked out just then with towels. One was a woman wearing a swimsuit, and the other was a man wearing boxers. They smiled at us as they passed, and we followed them up the path to the house.

Max, Amber, and I got into our respective vehicles and continued down the lane to the main gathering. We parked at the designated area before heading to the meadow.

Past wooden pasture fencing, an expanse of green grass skirted by wildflowers sat as the main feature of this part of the property. The valley nestled us into its lush embrace, with trees abundantly reaching up the hillsides and surrounding us with a buffer from the world beyond.

"This place is beautiful!" I said, admiring my surroundings.

"Just wait for the classes! I heard they've been absolutely incredible in previous gatherings," Maxille replied.

"I'm anticipating the Qi Gong offering on our last day will be the most popular," Amber predicted as she caught up with us.

The large canvas tent appeared to be the kitchen and eating area, with a few picnic tables under the outer awning. We climbed or ducked under the pasture fencing and made our way to the canvas tent.

Within it were several cushions haphazardly set out into circles. There were a few people already occupying one cluster, so we quickly got into line for our dinner and found another set of cushions to eat our curried lentils and chickpeas, and hearty quinoa salad. Amber mentioned that all the food prepared was vegetarian in honour of Ahimsa, the yogic principle of non-harming.

A couple of other gatherers came to sit down with us and joined our conversation.

"I think our spirits reincarnate," I overheard a boy with dark hair say to Amber as I was finishing my bowl.

"I think we just... cease," I spoke up.

"You really don't believe there's anything awaiting us in the afterlife? What if this *is* the afterlife and we just don't remember what came before?" he challenged.

"I think we have yet to advance our understanding of Spirit, or the soul well enough to know for certain what happens. So for now... I believe in this life that I am living and nothing more."

The boy laughed at me. He took another bite of his meal. "I agree with you that science needs to get with the program. Humans have advanced their knowledge of Spirit across many cultures and periods of our history. We just keep forgetting, or being told not to believe."

I smiled. This was my kind of conversation.

"I'm Hallie," I reached my hand across the small circle to introduce myself.

"Evan," he said and grinned back at me with a hint of mischief.

When dinner was finished, I went to look at the class schedule posted on the side of the tent. In a few hours, there would be an opening meditation. I was interested in a Vinyasa class tomorrow as well as the Qi Gong Amber had mentioned on Sunday. There was also a Kundalini class and a Pranayama workshop. The last offering was a closing meditation in the meadow.

"Which one are you looking forward to most?" Maxille asked me over my shoulder.

I shrugged before pointing to the closing meditation. "This one. Because after that, I go back to my life and hopefully it's a brand new path for me."

The four of us—including our new friend Evan—went up to the barn where the opening meditation was going to be held.

The loft of the barn was a significant, expansive space with beautiful murals of the flower of life, crows, the face of Buddha, and temples against the sunset. There were Buddhist prayer flags strung across the width of the barn in the front and back. The floor was raw, worn wooden planks that held remnants of a blue paint, long worn away.

Again, there were small groups of people scattered throughout the large area, waiting for the gathering to formally begin.

Evan wandered off to another group while Amber, Max, and I were left to catch up.

Amber and I bonded closely. As I started discussing my recent birthday trip, it turned out Amber and I were born just four days apart, making us a pair of Gemini's.

"Twins!" we joked with each other.

"Do you know your Ascendant?" Amber asked.

"Uh, no. I don't know what an Ascendant is," I replied. I had not studied much astrology though it had been on my mind to look into it further.

"Your Ascendant is the sign on the eastern horizon at the time you were born. It's also called your Rising Sign, because it's the sign of the sunrise!"

I was fascinated and also impressed that Amber already held some of this knowledge. "Have you used Tarot Cards before?"

"I LOVE Tarot! I left my deck at home, but I use it often."

I began to tell her of the card reading I had experienced with Nicole. I had brought my deck with me and I pulled it out of my bag. Amber admired the greyscale artistry. "The Eight of Swords was significant to me in her reading. When I did a pull the other day this card jumped out of the deck."

I showed her the Eight of Swords card.

"A butterfly!" Amber exclaimed.

Max nudged us then. I had been so caught in conversation that I hadn't noticed the loft of the barn had filled and a set of singing bowls was now set up in the corner.

Amber and I pulled away from each other slightly and shuffled into a comfortable seat.

Maverick started to speak and everyone went silent. "Welcome to the Summer Solstice Gathering! I'd like all of you to make yourselves at home here."

There were a few housekeeping items, like meal times and necessary facilities, but otherwise he turned the attention over to a woman who I recognized as a yoga teacher in the city.

"Please know that this is a very powerful time to be gathering," the woman began. "I want you all to be in your full expression of Spirit this weekend. Be yourself. Do not be afraid to do precisely what feels right to you."

She led us in a simple meditation, the kind that asked us to watch our thoughts and acknowledge them without judgement. She played the singing bowls which aided in a feeling of ethereal levity as I sat on the wooden floor of the barn.

I thought a lot about my explosive comments earlier in the day. I also thought about the unknown and where I might land in the next few months. I knew nothing of where this calling was taking me except in September I would begin a yoga teacher training.

My mind would drift and then I would bring my consciousness back to the blank space behind my eyes.

It was like a game. The moment I noticed the enchanting sound of the singing bowls, or remembered where I was, I was able to reel in my thoughts. My mind would wander, but I continued attempting to return it to centre.

Our teacher closed the meditation with an Ohm.

Her voice carried the first second of sound before others joined in a harmonious hum. My own lips parted to add to the collective sound. The volume of our voices swelled. "OH..."

The sound was deep, rich, resonant. The pitch began low, then shifted upwards as we attuned ourselves. The communal wave of this tonal adjustment brought us into the next part of the sacred sound.

"...mmm," I lingered in the vibrations of the room. It felt like time paused for only a moment, softly holding me in this state of peace before slowly the harmony began to fade.

I was at the end of my breath and softly let the hum in my chest fall quiet.

There was a moment of silence, stillness, hush I languished in before the teacher began to speak.

"Goodnight, farewell, take rest," she said. "I bid you all a safe return to your beds and a restful sleep tonight. There is much to take in tomorrow."

Many people dispersed. Evan returned to where us girls sat and joined us for conversation before we all decided it was late and bed sounded like an excellent place to be.

The fairy lights made our tent glow against the navy sky.

Maxille and I snuggled our sleeping bags into the centre of the tent. I fell asleep quickly to the sound of water flowing in the nearby stream.

The noise of Maxille rustling in her sleeping bag woke me in the morning.

I yawned as I asked, "Did you sleep well?"

Max was pulling articles of clothes into her sleeping bag with her. "I slept okay but would suggest dressing in layers this morning. Its chilly."

I sat up in my sleeping bag, leaning over my duffel to gather both shorts and long pants, a tank top, and a sweater. Following Max's lead, I pulled the items in logical order into the warmth of my sleeping bag and awkwardly donned my attire for the day.

When finished, my hands worked to secure my hair down the centre of my crown to the nape of my neck and as far beyond as I could go in a French braid.

Lastly, I gathered my mat, blocks, and strap into my backpack, along with my dishware, journal, pen, and tarot cards.

"Layers on," I told Max who appeared ready to greet the day.

"Rock on, let's go get some brekkie?" she suggested.

"Let's," I lifted my backpack up and unzipped the tent for us, putting on my shoes that were within the outer fly before unzipping the final threshold and emerging into the daylight.

For the early hour, it was rather bright and my eyes squinted at the clearing before me.

The small forest glade was an especially vivid green, and the canopy of leaves above rustled in the wind. The river and morning dew carried a freshness in the air which inherently raised my outlook of the day.

Maxille and I headed up the hill, past the steam hut, and down the lane toward the kitchen tent. There were other gatherers headed to or from the same direction, and smiles were exchanged when paths crossed.

When we reached the kitchen tent, we pulled out our dishware, reserved seats with our backpacks, and got in line for breakfast.

Tofu scramble with peppers and onion, toast, and hash browns were available this morning. I took a little of each and poured some coffee from a large percolator into my tumbler.

Max and I returned to our backpacks and began to eat, both still appearing to be overcome by a morning haze.

"The Vinyasa is first this morning," I overheard a girl speaking behind us. "It's in the loft."

"Which classes did you want to attend today?" I asked Max, attempting conversation.

"All of them if I can," she said. "What about you?"

"I haven't looked, but I'm impartial. The Vinyasa does sound like a great place to start thou—." My reply was interrupted by a sizable crash within the kitchen space.

Several people got up to assist with what appeared to be an overturned serving dish.

Max and I laughed, assessing the situation and determining it to be well in hand. We were, however, both finished and waited until the commotion had dispersed before getting up to wash our dishes at the back of the tent.

We returned our dishes to our packs before navigating through the other gatherers enjoying their breakfast and out into the meadow.

As we made our way to the barn, a small black and white spotted cat crossed our path, brushing up against Max's leg.

"She's just had kittens!" Max seemed certain.

"How do you know?" I asked.

"I overheard some of the gatherers talking about kittens somewhere." She started peering around the barn. Two women came out of one of the horses stalls, smiling.

"There!" Maxille beelined it for the stall.

"Keep the door closed so the dogs don't get in," one of the girls who had just left mentioned.

I nodded, myself and the spotted cat following Max into the stall. I closed the door and turned around upon hearing several high pitched and tiny mews begin to sound.

Little black kittens seemed to appear out of nowhere, greeting us at the door.

"Oh my goodness," Max said softly as she sat down and waited for the kittens to come to her.

I watched as a few of the tiny balls of fluff started climbing onto her lap and smiled.

The mother cat was circling my legs, meowing loudly.

I picked up the spotted female and held her in my arms. "Are these your babies?"

She meowed again.

"You did a very good job, momma." I pet the top of her head.

Maxille was petting the kittens who had come to her, picking one up and giving it a kiss on the nose.

"Are you happy?" I asked Max.

"So happy!" she exclaimed. "I want one."

People were opening the door to the stall.

"We heard there were kittens," they said.

Maxille gave three of them final kisses on the top of their heads before getting up. I put momma cat down and vacated the stall to make room for the new visitors.

"Make sure you keep the door shut," Max instructed. "Apparently the dogs are unkind."

The small group of people nodded as we exchanged places and shut the stall door behind us.

We made our way up to the loft through a set of stairs at the front of the barn. A number of gatherers had already set up their mats sporadically throughout the space.

Maxille led the way to a spot under the Buddha's face. Both of us laid down our mats and just for good measure I also pulled out my blocks and strap.

Once set up, I lay with my eyes closed, tuning out the sounds of the room.

Riggley's sweet face came to mind.

I missed him fiercely already, and even more so considering I may never see him again. My opportunity to say goodbye had been overshadowed by my anger, and I missed my chance.

The grief of this knowledge settled deep in my heart, weighing my breath and flushing my face with distress.

After everything we had been through. All the work I had put into training him. All the walks, the tricks taught, the memories shared with the girls upstairs.

The longing to keep him in my world built with an intensity I could not keep contained.

He was not mine. He was not mine. He was not mine.

Tears streamed down my face, wetting the little hairs which had not found their place in my braid that morning.

"Hello, welcome," the same teacher from last night's meditation spoke from the stairs of the loft.

She made her way to a mat at the front of the barn, the one perpendicular to the rest of the class. I wiped my face with my hands as I rose to a seat.

"This is going to be a very heart-opening Vinyasa, so prepare yourselves for backbends today." Her voice carried easily throughout the space.

"Please begin in child's pose, making space between your knees to allow your heart to sink deeply toward the floor," she instructed.

I moved to a kneeling position, hinging at the hips to bow into the floor with my arms outstretched.

"Stay here for just a moment, perhaps inching your fingertips farther forward to allow your chest to expand."

I followed the suggestion, moving my fingertips forward as far as they would go.

I'm done with you!

The damage done from those words was entirely irreparable. They acted as a severance of my relationship with Jordan. An ending that held finality.

"We're going to move into a salutation, so in your own time please move into a standing position," our teacher guided us.

I lifted myself with my hands and slowly moved into standing.

"Inhale, rise."

I extended my arms above my head, letting my hands touch, taking a breath in.

"Exhale, fold."

I let my torso fall, my hands catching me when they reached the ground while I let my breath out.

"Inhale, halfway lift."

My hands raised to my thighs as I straighten my back. Breath in.

"Exhale, fold."

Hands returned to the floor, letting my fingertips touch my mat. Breath out.

"Inhale, step or jump back into an engaged plank."

I planted my palms to the floor and shot my feet out behind me, activating my abdominals to hold the position in good alignment.

"Exhale, lower."

Keeping my core engaged, I kept my elbows close to my body as I lowered to hover before my chest and chin touched the floor.

"Inhale, upward dog."

I pressed my hands into the mat as I lifted my chest to the front of the room, arching my back and straightening my arms.

"We will hold here for three breaths. Let them be deep and moving."

I took my first breath in, letting air fill my lungs.

As I breathed out, the rawness of my emotional state started to surface.

I took a shaky breath in, my heart sinking with grief that clutched my chest. I let the breath out, bowing my head as the flush rose to my face again.

Breath in, I lifted my tear-streaked face to the room. Breath out, I let my shoulders engage and align into a stronger posture.

"Allow your hips to lead you back into downward dog. We will spend three breaths here."

Again, I pressed my palms downward and raised my hips into the pose. The stretch made my hamstrings tense and blood rush to my head as I looked at my knees and took my breaths.

One, my relationship was over.

Two, I would never see my dog again.

Three, I was grieving. It would be okay.

Again and again, as our teacher guided us through standing postures she would give us three breaths to hold the pose. Low lunge with cactus arms, then a twist. Triangle pose. Dancer. The first breath I was rocked by insurmountable pain gripping my heart. The second, maintained distress. The third breath, a resolve to not let it overcome me.

I cycled through the emotions, again and again until our teacher led us to the floor.

"We are going to be preparing for wheel pose, so find yourselves on your back and we will begin in little bridge."

Moving to lay down, I stared at the vaulted beams supporting the ceiling of the loft.

I couldn't undo the experiences I'd had. I couldn't undo the words I had said. I was on the cusp of a new beginning, and there was no going back. The only way my soul could go was onward.

New determination overcame me.

"Inhale, bend your knees, and lift your hips, allowing your hands to find each other beneath you."

I did as instructed, my shoulders hugging each other as I clasped my hands with straight arms beneath me. I raised my hips as high as they would go as I focused my gaze on a beam.

One, I could do this.

Two, there was a great adventure waiting for me.

Three, my destiny was unfolding.

"Exhale, lower your hips."

Letting myself fall back to the ground, I relaxed as I breathed out.

"Inhale, one more and then we will move into wheel."

I repeated the posture.

One, calm.

Two, peace.

Three, all was okay.

"Exhale, return to the floor."

My body relaxed into my mat.

"Now, put your hands at the tops of your shoulders, fingers pointing to feet. Inhale, push into your hands, and raise your chest upwards into wheel."

This was a challenging pose for me as I didn't have the flexibility in my shoulders to reach full extension. I put my blocks at the top of my shoulders and placed my hands on them before putting all my strength into raising myself into wheel.

"Three breaths, class. It will feel challenging, but I promise it will be worth your effort."

One, gaze between hands.

Two, an extra press to straighten my arms.

Three, hold. I was strong here.

"Release your wheel and lay back now. Bring your knees to your chest."

I gingerly let my shoulders return to the mat and my hips followed. I folded my knees into my chest and wrapped my arms around them.

"When you are ready, you may return your feet to the floor and slide them out to find yourselves in corpse pose. We are nearly ready to close this class." Our teacher sat in the centre of her mat, overlooking the class who was now settling into the final resting pose.

"As you continue through this gathering, remember to embrace the feelings that may have risen during your practice. There is strength to be found in the emotions guiding our decisions. Honour the sensations, thoughts, impulses, within you and take action where necessary to find yourself on the path your Soul desires to walk." Her words carried over the class with a wisdom I was now also wise to. I was living it. It was a friend to me.

We lay in silence for several minutes before our teacher invited us to a seat. Her hands were already set in prayer at her heart.

"May the divine light in me, see the divine light in you. Namaste." She bowed her head to the floor, the class following like the tide going out to sea.

As we, in our own time rose from our bows, everyone began rustle and stir with movement.

"I saw you were letting the feelings flow." Max leaned over her mat to embrace me in a hug.

I hugged her back tightly and said, "the tears came on strong, but so did the strength."

It was good to be surrounded by friends. The Universe was supporting me by gifting me this weekend. I was fully embraced here.

We collected our things and as we were walking out of the barn, Max and I ran into Amber and Evan. They were talking animatedly and laughing outside the entrance.

"Hello, hello!" Max sang.

"Oh! Hello, you two!" The corners of Amber's eyes pinched. "Would either of you kindly care to skip class and come to the river with us?"

I looked at Max. She looked up toward the loft. "There's the Kundalini class next that I was really looking forward to!"

"Hallie?" Amber asked.

I hesitated. Maxille had invited me and I didn't want to leave her if she wanted my company. "What's at the river?"

"Friends." Amber grinned.

"Go, Hallie," Max nudged. "We're going to be spending so much time together soon. If you want to go, you should."

"You sure?"

"Yes! Go!" Max laughed.

I gave Maxille a big hug with a gentle squeeze. "Enjoy the Kundalini. Tell me about it after!"

"Can do!"

Amber gave me a gentle shoulder check as we walked away from the barn. "Spending more time together, hey?"

I laughed. "She's soon to be my new roomie!"

"Oh! That's awesome. You two are so compatible!" Amber smiled.

"She seems like someone who knows how to cook. You're lucky," Evan pitched in.

I smiled. "We haven't negotiated dinner arrangements yet, but I bet she does!"

We walked for a while down the path, chatting inconsequentially. I was beginning to sense a mutual interest between Amber and Evan but I didn't want to call it out, or interfere. I allowed myself to simply notice.

When we arrived at the river, there were already a handful who had gathered.

Amber greeted them and introduced me. I lost several names as soon as I heard them but smiled back politely and took a seat on the cleanest and largest looking rock. I recognized a familiar face.

The man from the metaphysical shop was there. I hadn't noticed him at the opening ceremony last night. As I looked at his face, our eyes caught.

He smiled. I nodded in acknowledgment.

Once I sat down, I noticed most of the gatherers had instruments of some sort. Shakers. A wooden flute. A guitar.

Evan sat next to me and asked if the guitar could be passed to him.

"Are we beginning then?" a dreadlock-laden man asked as he passed Evan the guitar.

I shot a curious glance at Amber who was smiling.

"If you are ready," Amber declared.

Evan started to strum on the guitar, testing it.

The guy with the dreadlocks offered me the shakers but I shook my head. "I'll clap!"

In some unspoken upbeat, the person who had taken up the flute began to play a slow, soothing melody.

Evan joined in with a few chords on the guitar, the shakers held by the man from the metaphysical shop started shifting, Dreadlocks was thumping on their backpack, and Amber began to hum harmonious tunes.

I had just joined an impromptu jam and I was loving it. I added my claps where I thought they were appropriate and swayed where I sat.

Those moments held my full presence.

I wasn't thinking about Jordan or the unknown. My only thoughts were my next clap and how beautiful the river was.

The tune slowly shifted into different chords and a new melody. The rest of us changed our beats and patterns, accepting the challenge of bringing everyone into harmony.

I had never in my life experienced such oneness with strangers. I wasn't sure if it was the place or the atmosphere or the presence of like-minded people but I felt content. Blissful, even.

Evan played a few closing notes before everyone else allowed their role to fade into silence. We sat for a while, with only the sound of the stream beside us and a few bird calls to listen to. The quiet was a juxtaposition to the music we created, but it was welcome nonetheless.

The silence was broken by a few other gatherers joining us. I smiled in greeting.

"We heard the music! It was like a beacon calling us!" one of them said.

Conversation and chattering resumed. I sat on my rock, looking out over the river. Words of poetry stirred in my mind, yet I could hardly grasp them with the socialization surrounding me.

I turned to Amber. "Do you mind if I take off? This was lovely."

"Of course not! Go! Be free! Enjoy whatever you choose to do next." Amber gave me a squeeze on the shoulder.

I gave her and Evan parting smiles before following the path to the river back to the place where it forked toward our tents.

I was able to find our camping spot easily and unzipped the outer canvas. Carefully taking off my wet shoes, and awkwardly balancing on top of them, I unzipped the inner tent and fell into the squishy softness of our sleeping bags and blankets.

My first moment of solitude since arriving in the valley brought a desire for reflection.

Finding my journal within my backpack I shuffled off and lodged in the corner of the tent, I sat on my side of the bedding in silence.

I could already tell my thoughts were not as chaotic as yesterday or even earlier today.

Instead of writing now, a pull toward my cards diverted my attention. I could journal after the pull. Fortunately, I found my deck within the backpack also. I turned on the fairy lights and then sat for quite some time with the cards held loosely in my hands, taking deep breaths and finding my centre.

I wanted to know what came next. I wanted to ask the cards what calling was so significant for this to have all transpired?

I whispered a prayer before pulling the cards, then looked to the top of the tent, asking the heavens for clarity.

Honouring my past, honouring my present, looking into the future, I call in my spirit guides to show me the way.

I pulled a single card to act as a focus, and then another three for past, present, and future.

The Focus: KING OF SWORDS
A calling.
To a cause of significance which will affect many.

The Past: THE SUN [REVERSED]
Challenging circumstances.
You may have felt hopeless.

The Present: KING OF WANDS
Leadership.
It is time to lead the way forward into new horizons.

The Future: NINE OF WANDS
Grit.
Resilience will be required as confidence wanes at the final stand.

As I read the meanings of the cards the message sunk in deeply. I was meant to accomplish something of significance and weight. I was being called. To what? I still wasn't sure the cards outlined it clearly, but something told me I would be acting in my power to overcome new feats. To do something I may never have thought possible for me without this newfound freedom.

I wanted to *create*. I wanted to *offer*. I wanted to *grow*.

I wrote the cards and their associated meanings into my journal. As I was close to finishing, I heard the cracking of twigs under foot.

The outer canvas of the tent unzipped.

"Hi Max," I called out.

"Hi! What are you up to?" Max asked as she entered the tent. "Oh!" She noticed the cards in front of me. "Tarot time!"

I nodded. "I just read for myself. It's clear that I have a new chapter ahead of me."

"That's a good thing! Also quite accurate—you do have a new adventure ahead!" Max confirmed.

"Have you eaten dinner yet?" I asked.

"No! Want to go?"

"Please! I'm hungry!" Almost on cue, my stomach rumbled as if to make a point.

"Noted! Let me grab a heavier jacket and we can go!"

I collected the cards and returned them to my deck as Maxille ruffled through her bags.

Max waited until we were out of the tent before putting her jacket on.

I asked about her Kundalini class as we were on our way to dinner. She started talking about 'Jupiter fingers' and other breathwork techniques. I realized I was glad I skipped it to go to the river and read my cards, but still happy she enjoyed her class.

We found ourselves at the kitchen tent where veggie burgers were being served. We got in line and I told Maxille what she had missed at the river.

"A river jam? Incredible!" she exclaimed.

One of the karma servers assisting with the meal preparation overheard our conversation and pitched in.

"We could hear it from here," they said. "It was lovely!"

I agreed. It was lovely. It was also neat how it had affected other people.

Max and I sat together in a clear area of cushions and started eating as other gatherers began to filter in.

"Thank you," I said to Max after a moment.

"Oh! For what?"

"For the invitation. I couldn't have imagined a better weekend." I truly felt grateful that I was in a positive environment instead of at home alone, ruminating.

"Oh, my sweet Hallie. Of course! I wanted you to be here. And it's good for you. Cheers to friendship!" She lifted her water bottle.

"Cheers!" We heard behind us.

As I looked over my shoulder Evan was approaching with a plate, smiling.

"Cheers, Max." I lifted my glass as Evan sat down.

"Where did you run off to, Hallie?" he asked.

"To my tent. For some much needed Hallie-time!" I took another bite of my burger.

"Hallie-time! I love it." I heard Amber's voice before I noticed her presence. She took a seat next to Evan, leaving Max and I sitting a half-circle away from each other.

"Are we all going to Qi Gong tomorrow?" I asked.

"Planning on it!"

"I am!"

"Yes!"

The affirmations were said simultaneously.

"Wear something comfortable tomorrow," Amber offered. "You'll want to be free to move."

"Have you done it before?" I asked.

"No, but that's the advice I was given yesterday so I'm passing it along." She smiled.

I laughed. "Thanks!"

We all finished our meals and washed our dishes.

As we left the kitchen tent, the sunset had struck the clouds in beautiful pink and orange tones with the deepest blue threatening the edge of the sky.

"So pretty!" Max noted my gaze.

"Isn't it?" I murmured.

We all stuck together for the remainder of the evening, having conversations by the fire and eventually testing out the steam hut to warm up before bed.

Something told me that tomorrow would bring a new revelation. I was certain this weekend would leave me with a gift before we parted ways.

I Am a Leader

I woke in the morning warm and cozy in my sleeping bag. My nose, though, still felt the cold of the night so I tucked my face in under the edge of the covers to shake the chill.

Max had snuggled in during the night and was just starting to open her eyes.

"Mornin's," I mumbled.

"What time is it?"

I fumbled looking for my phone. "8:18."

"Breakfast time!" Max started to sit up slowly.

The Qi Gong class didn't start for another hour so we had a little bit of time, but I was awake now and wanted to join the community.

I gathered my clothes and snuck them into my sleeping bag again so I could change out of my pyjamas without being exposed.

Max held a mirror as she brushed fresh mascara on. She offered the mirror when she was done. "You should do a braid!"

I took a look at myself. The suggestion must be Maxille's kindest way of letting me know my hair was a frazzled mess.

"Oh goodness," I sighed as I shuffled through my bag looking for a brush.

I found it near the bottom of the duffel and began to temper the tousle before starting another French braid.

When I finally felt presentable, I unzipped the side of my sleeping bag and stretched.

"Ready?" Max asked.

"Yes! Let's go get some breakfast." I moved toward the entrance of the tent.

As I stepped out into the cool morning air, I could hear rustles from Amber's tent next to ours.

"Good morning!" I called out.

"Good morning!"

"Would you like us to wait?"

"No go ahead, I'll be a moment." Amber urged us along.

Max crawled out of the tent. "It's crisp out here!"

Sunlight streamed through the trees above us. The air was slightly humid from the morning dew which coated the grass and the undersides of the leaves hovering over the tent.

Max and I started our small trek back to the meadow, both yawning and moving slowly as we went.

Breakfast included yogurt, granola, and warm oatmeal with berries. Amber joined us as one of the karma servers announced a fresh batch of coffee was ready.

"Do you have your tumbler? Would you like a fill?" she asked as she approached Maxille and I.

I lifted mine. "Yes, please."

Amber took my tumbler as she passed and filled both hers and mine before returning the vessel back to me.

"This has been such a wonderful weekend. I'm sad to pack up," Amber sighed.

Her comment instantly brought me back into the awareness that my life would start anew once I got home. I had almost been able to forget since waking, but now the fact returned to my mind.

Almost on cue, Max looked at me. "Let me know if there's any drama when you get home, Hallie."

"I'm not sure what I'll be going home to," I said honestly. "I appreciate the offer."

My anxiety sparked. After such a heated argument before I left, I wondered how Jordan would behave when I returned. Perhaps the house would be empty when I arrived. Perhaps there would be awkwardness and more anger to endure.

This was the precise reason why I was afraid of the breakup. The anger. The heartbreak. The hurt. I knew that the only way out of this was through, but it was still awful to know that I caused such pain.

"Earth to Hallie." Amber waved at me.

"Sorry." I jolted out of my thoughts. "I was just thinking about going home. I've decided I'd like to stay here forever."

"Wouldn't we all!" Amber agreed.

It was almost time for the Qi Gong class. I got up to look at the class schedule to see where we were supposed to meet.

"Qi Gong? You coming?" I heard Evan ask behind me. He had been stealthy in his approach.

"I think all of us are," I said, "Just looking for where to meet."

"Right here!" The guy with the dreadlocks from the river yesterday was standing beside Evan. "I'm hosting the class."

"Oh, hello!" I reached out my hand. "I'm Hallie, we met at the river."

"I remember." He took my hand firmly and gave it a single shake. "Einar."

The name clicked. I remembered its uniqueness during the introductions at the river but it had been too foreign for me to catch it for keeps.

"Einar. I'm excited for your class!" My hand was returned to me.

Amber and Max had stood up and joined our little circle around the schedule.

"Shall we step out of the way?" I asked, noticing others were intending to look at the class list also.

Einar led us outside of the canvas tent where we formed a new circle and other gatherers began to join us. Quiet chatter kept us company as the class convened, and after a moment or two, it appeared as though we had everyone.

"Take off your shoes if you would like. Feeling the earth against your soles is soothing to our souls. This way." Einar started up the hill.

I removed my shoes and followed Einar and the rest of the group into the woods. The mossy earth sent stabbing and sharp sensations through my feet on some steps and a cushioned, soft experience on others.

Once we were deep into the woods and had lost sight of the clearing, Einar asked us to spread out. I chose a spot in a bed of soft moss.

For a moment, I lost myself admiring the haze of morning humidity. It cast visible, purling currents in the rays of sunlight slipping around the shadows of branch and gatherer.

"Find a place where your feet feel connected to the ground. Lift your shoulders, pull them back, then let them fall. Close your eyes." Einar's voice interrupted my distraction. The sound was gravelly but soothing.

I straightened my spine and allowed my eyelids to fall.

"Qi Gong is the movement of energy within an active breathing meditation. The motion of the body alongside visualization of energy makes the practice powerful. Our first step is to feel the energy.

"Extend your hands far out to the side, stretching out your wingspan. Feel or imagine the energy between your right fingertips and your left."

The feeling was diffuse, subtle but there.

"Now slowly press your hands together and sense when the energy begins to resist."

My hands did not get past my shoulders before they could not move closer together. My eyes opened, perplexed. I could *feel* the energy. It was not budging, the resistance was tangible.

I closed my eyes again as Einar continued.

"This orb is your Qi. Take a moment to feel its boundaries. Revolve your hands around it, feel its edges."

My hands treated the orb as though it was a globe, spinning and flipping it in front of me. Imagining the ball of energy, I saw that it was golden and glowing.

"Now, with both hands, press the orb into your heart and allow its energy to expand within your ribcage. As you breathe in, lift your hands to the level of your crown chakra and feel the orb rise as well. As you breathe out, push your hands down to the level of your root chakra and feel the orb follow. Maintain resistance with your Qi and continue to move the energy up and down your spine with your breath."

I lifted my arms and imagined I was moving Qi up and down my backbone.

After two or three cycles, the air around me shifted into a tangible weight on my skin. I was becoming formless, the boundaries of my body beginning to meld with my environment and yet I could still firmly feel my feet anchoring me to the ground.

There was silence between the trees and the class. The occasional chirp of a songbird. The soft rush of wind far in the distance.

As I relaxed deeply and continued the practice, something within my back clicked.

I heard the sound.

At the level of my solar plexus, my spine straightened. Merenya's reading came to mind. My energy must have rebalanced as I now stood taller, more aligned.

Had I reclaimed my personal power over this weekend? By finally being alone I would no longer be giving my power away, but standing strong by myself.

I let out the longest exhale.

Finally. I was free.

Einar allowed the class to continue for another few minutes before softly calling for us to press our hands against our hearts firmly and seal the energy.

I stayed with my eyes closed and my hands on my chest even after I heard the rustles of the class moving and starting to leave.

A hand on my shoulder finally allowed me to return to the forest.

"You look at peace." Max smiled at me.

"I am. Thank you for leading me here this weekend." I rested my hand on hers. "Truly, it was exactly what I needed."

"Happy that is the case!" Maxille bounced. "Time to pack up the tent?"

Ah yes, the tent.

"Let's go!"

There was an hour until the closing meditation. Max and I efficiently packed our things, disassembled the tent, and attempted to fold and return it to its bag. We didn't do a very good job.

As we were hauling the partially open and overflowing tent bag back up the hill to the car, Amber caught up with us to take her own site down.

"I hope we stay in touch over the summer!" She continued down toward her tent a few steps as she spoke.

"That would be lovely," Max said. "Lets try to make a point of it!"

I nodded. "Yes, let's! Do you need any help?"

"No, Evan is about to come this way. He needed to grab a few things from the kitchen. Be free!" Amber smiled and waved goodbye.

I returned the gesture and continued up the hill.

We stuffed the tent bag into the car and headed to the meadow.

Every gatherer from the weekend was slowly trickling into the meadow, smiling and making small pockets of conversation. I laid down my folded mat as a seat next to Max and closed my eyes.

I reflected deeply on my entire experience, from the Shamanic Journey until today. It had been a difficult path to travel, with many emotions rising to the surface.

Fear.

Hope.

Faith.

I felt a soft flutter on my hand and opened my eyes. A moth had landed on the edge of my mat. I stared for a moment in wonder, looking intently at the creature. Its tan-toned fluffy body appeared soft and velvety. The markings on its wings would be perfect camouflage against the tree trunks surrounding the meadow.

I slowly lowered my hand and allowed the little moth to climb onto my palm. I brought her closer to my face, admiring her lovingly.

"Oh, my. Hallie!" Amber arrived behind me, witnessing the moment.

She rested her hands on my shoulders and joined my gaze. I looked up at Amber. Her eyes widened with amazement then softened in awe of the moment. She smiled before leaving my side to take her seat.

Maverick began calling the meadow to quiet, and I settled the little moth to rest on the right side of my chest.

"It is with a sadness in my heart that we must close the Gathering for this weekend. Celebrating the Summer Solstice with you all has been a blessing and a treat!" His voice carried over the cluster of gatherers.

"The theme of this final meditation is to remember that our words through intentions have power. The seeds we plant in this season will come to fruit over the next nine years. Be prepared that the words which come to you today will set the tone for the decade to come.

"Be still, now. Allow your wisdom to come to you. Uncover the alignment with your future in this moment."

I sat in stillness.

The rustle of wind stirred fine hairs to tickled my face. The cool, fresh scent of the meadow's flora filled my senses. The sound of trees brushing against each other calmed me.

I sat.

Still.

Waiting.

The words came into my mind almost as though the wind delivered them itself.

"*I am a Leader. What is my work? I want to give.*"

A sudden tightness developed in my chest. Tighter than the anxiety I felt all winter and spring, this sensation gripped my heart with an excited anticipation of the path ahead.

If my intuition acted a north star, then it was navigating the way with its whispers. From now onward I would listen and allow it to guide me as I uncovered my calling.

I am a Leader.

I had always wanted to be.

Lifting the moth from my chest, I cradled her in my hands. The little creature began fluttering her wings before taking off and floating across the meadow.

This wasn't the end, only a final chapter. An entirely new story awaited me:

a mission to follow my intuition.

@authorakbird
www.authorakbird.com